Buddhism for Beginners:

How The Practice of Buddhism, Mindfulness and Meditation Can Increase Your Happiness and Help You Deal With Stress and Anxiety

Copyright Notice

No part of this book may be reproduced or transmitted in any form whatsoever, electronic, or mechanical, including photocopying, recording, or by any information storage or retrieval system without expressed written, dated and signed permission from the author. All copyrights are reserved.

Disclaimer

Reasonable care has been taken to ensure that the information presented in this book is accurate. However, the reader should understand that the information provided does not constitute legal, medical or professional advice of any kind.

No Liability: this product is supplied "as is" and without warranties. All warranties, express or implied, are hereby disclaimed. Use of this product constitutes acceptance of the "No Liability" policy. If you do not agree with this policy, you are not permitted to use or distribute this product.

We shall not be liable for any losses or damages whatsoever (including, without limitation, consequential loss or damage) directly or indirectly arising from the use of this product.

A SPIRITUAL START!

Start your week with gratitude, joy, inspiration, and love.

Healing, motivation, inspiration, challenge and guidance straight to your inbox every week!

FIND OUT MORE

Contents:

Introduction

Chapter 1 – The Foundations of Buddhism

Chapter 2 - The 5 Precepts – Buddha's Guide to a Simple Life

Chapter 3 - The Three Marks of Existence of Buddha

Chapter 4 - Karma and Zen in Buddhism

Chapter 5 - Ethics and Other Vital Things in Buddhism

Chapter 6 - Start Your Spiritual Path

Chapter 7 – Training The Mind With Meditation

Chapter 8 - Different Kinds of Meditation

Chapter 9 - Cultivating Mindfulness

Chapter 10 – Yoga and Buddhism

Chapter 11 - The Mudras and Basic Poses in Yoga

Chapter 12- Mastering Yoga Poses

Chapter 13 – How to Relax and Meditate Through Yoga

Chapter 14 – Center Yourself With Sound Healing

Chapter 15 - Vibrational Healing

Chapter 16 - Healing Instruments

Conclusion

Introduction

Learning about Buddhism at this day and age will help you understand that there is more to life than what you see. You only have to go past the material things and luxuries to realize that you are more than your physical qualities, you are not your ego nor your mind.

The founder of Buddhism, Siddhartha Gautama Buddha, is the epitome of what this belief stands for. He grew up surrounded by luxuries, but he opted to turn his back on all the riches to contemplate and gain enlightenment.

This book outlines Buddha's teachings that will have a great impact on your life. It will help you gain a deeper understanding of life.

To help you towards your journey to enlightenment and self-realization, this book has detailed information about the different kinds of meditation practices you can learn to perform.

This book tells the story of Siddhartha and how he became the Buddha. You will learn a lot from his teachings and concepts he was able to spread to his disciples. It also has a useful guide about Zen meditation, yoga, sound healing, and the other forms of meditation you can do as a beginner in the practice.

Enjoy!

Chapter 1 – The Foundations of Buddhism

It is believed that Buddhism started more than 2,500 years ago in India. It was founded by Siddhartha Gautama, born to a clan of a tribal chief in Nepal. A soothsayer predicted when Siddhartha was born that he will be a renouncer. His father tried to prevent this by showering him with all the luxuries he can afford.

Siddhartha lived a sheltered life. But he came to a point that he started to question life. His curiosity of what lies beyond the palace walls prompted him to ask his father to let him go out and see the world. The young Siddhartha set out a series of chariot rides to go around. It was then that his eyes were opened to the "real" state of life – far from the pleasures, fortunes, and riches he has grown accustomed to.

During his travels, the young man was faced with extreme forms of human suffering like illness, old age, and death. He also met an ascetic renouncer.

The realizations opened the young Siddhartha's mind of life's simple truths he was deprived of knowing while growing up - people grow old, get sick, and die. At that point, he realized that all life's pleasures were fleeting and only hide human misery.

He decided to leave his wife and son and devoted his time to expanding his knowledge about his newfound truths.

He first tried following the monk's sample. He denied himself of the pleasures in life and started leading life of utmost asceticism. He also tried severe abandonment in the forest to the point of almost starving himself. It was not easy as it almost took his life. Until one day, he heard someone uttered something about the strings of a musical instrument - that you can't make beautiful music if the strings were too loose and if they were too tight, they will just snap.

After understanding that starvation only added to his suffering, he began eating and spent a lot of time sitting underneath a tree while meditating.

Reaching Nirvana

Several known versions exist today as to how the young Siddhartha reached his goal. There were accounts that said it happened the morning after, while there are others stating that Siddhartha found Nirvana (Enlightenment) 6 months after. He knew he had found the answers to why humans suffer and how to eliminate suffering.

Becoming the Buddha

Once Siddhartha achieved Enlightenment, he became known as the Buddha (also called the Awakened One or the Enlightened One).

The Buddha began his mission of ending all human suffering by teaching his truths. Not long after, he became popular and gained many followers.

His most important teachings were the Eight-Fold Path and the Four Noble Truths.

The Four Noble Truths

1. Life is dukkha (suffering).

2. Human suffering is brought about by craving – for pleasures and things to be, unfortunately they are not. It is a person's refusal to see life as it is that causes suffering.

3. There's an end to life's suffering.

4. The means to end life's sufferings – Middle Way and Eight-Fold Path.

The Middle Way

The Middle Way, a characterization of Buddha's life, suggests that people must not indulge their body's every whim but to not totally deny the physical body either. Upon following the combined path of the Middle Way and Eight-Fold Path should one attain Nirvana and experience utter joy and peace.

The Spread of Buddhism

When the Buddha died, his celibate and wandering followers settled down at monasteries provided by married laityas. To return the favor, these followers shared Buddha's important teachers to them. In return, the monks taught these laityas of the important teachings of Buddha. They visited the Buddha's birthplace, started to worship the tree where the Buddha received enlightenment, they put images of the Buddha in their temples, and placed his relics in different stupas (funeral mounds).

In the 3rd century BCE, Ashoka, a famous king, and his son spread and taught Buddhism throughout Ceylon (Sri Lanka) and South India.

From its original Indian foundation, Buddhism began to spread to various countries around the globe. Currently, the estimated Buddhist population around the world is about 500 million. Myanmar, Cambodia, and Thailand have the highest recorded percentages of this religion among all their residents while the largest Buddhist population is in China.

Buddhism is also gradually getting practitioners in the United Kingdom, Australia, and America.

Within Buddhism are many schools or division and two major branches, which vary in the areas of focus. Mahayana Buddhism concentrates on educating about the ways to enlightenment and joint freedom from suffering. Its two offshoots, Tibetan and Zen Buddhism are the kinds many people practice in western countries. Theravada Buddhism concentrates on monastic life and individual experience and enlightenment.

Nirvana

The term, which literally means quenching or blowing out, refers to the ultimate goal of the Buddhist path. It is included in the cessation of dukkha or the Third Truth in the Four Noble Truths. It is commonly interpreted as the extinguishing of the "three fires" that results in samsara or freedom from the cycle of rebirth. It is also associated with other Buddhism terms, such as the states of sunyata or emptiness and anatta or non-self.

Nirvana refers to the state when you become free from rebirth and suffering, although it was given different meanings in various Buddhist traditions.

Chapter 2 - The 5 Precepts — Buddha's Guide to a Simple Life

The five precepts cover the foundation of Buddhist training. Buddha knew it would be challenging to apply these precepts to all areas of your life every day but also understand their virtue towards reaching higher forms of wisdom and development. These precepts are also referred to as the noble eightfold path.

This is a guide to end human suffering found within the fourth noble truth. The path is categorized into three — wisdom, mental discipline, and moral conduct.

The Eight-Fold Path

1. Samma Samadhin — Right concentration

2. Samma Sati — Right mindfulness

3. Samma Vayama — Right effort

4. Samma Ajiva — Right livelihood

5. Samma Kammanta — Right action

6. Samma Vaca — Right speech

7. Samma Sankappa — Right thought

8. Samma Ditthi — Right understanding

The Eight-Fold Path in relation to the categories they belong to:

1. Wisdom

Right Understanding – This is said to be the highest form of wisdom that sees the Ultimate Reality or seeing things as they are. There are two kinds of understanding in Buddhism. Penetration or pativedha is deep understanding. It means that you see through things without any label or name. You see things beyond their impurities. You can only gain this kind of understanding through meditation. The other kind of understanding, which is not quite deep, is known as knowing accordingly or anubodha. This is how your mind perceives things based on the information given.

Right Thought – It encompasses the right thought of all beings, such as non-violence, love, and detachment or selfless renunciation. Lack of wisdom in any areas of life, such as political, social or individual, result in thoughts about violence, hatred, ill-will, and selfish desire.

2. Ethical conduct

Ethical conduct, also called sila, is based on the wide concept of compassion and universal love for all living things. This is said to be the basis of the teachings of Buddha. Buddhism believes that two qualities make a perfect man – wisdom or panna and compassion or karuna.

Compassion represents the noble qualities of the heart and emotion, such as tolerance, kindness, charity, and love. Wisdom represents the great qualities and intellectual side of the mind. A man has to have balanced wisdom and compassion. Too much intellect without compassion may lead to becoming a genius but hard-hearted individual and too much compassion without wisdom may result in becoming a good-hearted fool. Compassion and wisdom are linked and inseparable in Buddhism.

Here are the three factors of the noble eightfold path included in ethical conduct:

Right Speech – It means refraining from saying harmful and wrong speech, such as:

- Gossip, and foolish, useless, and idle babble
- Abusive, malicious, impolite, rude, and harsh language
- Slander and backbiting and talk that could cause disharmony, disunity, enmity, and hatred among groups of people or individuals
- Telling lies

It means that one has to be careful when speaking. It is better to keep noble silence than to say anything unpleasant or hurtful. One has to speak the truth all the time and has to use words, which are useful, meaningful, gentle, pleasant, and friendly.

Right Action – It teaches people to stay away from dishonorable conducts, such as illegitimate sexual encounters, dishonest dealings, stealing, and destroying other people's lives. It prompts individuals to lead an honorable and peaceful life by following a moral compass.

Right Livelihood – It reflects the strong opposition of Buddhism to the use and trading of lethal weapons and arms and any kind of war. It teaches people to stay away from sources of income that may cause harm to others, which include cheating, killing, selling poison and intoxicating drinks and trading lethal weapons. A person should earn a living through means that won't cause harm to others, blameless and honorable.

3. Mental Discipline

Right Effort – Teaches people to find balance in cultivating enthusiasm and positive attitude. It should produce an attitude of cheerful yet steady determination. Human beings should cultivate clear and honest thoughts and do away with negative and jealous feelings to produce right effort.

Right effort simply equates positive thinking.

Right Mindfulness – It teaches people to be attentive, mindful, and diligently aware of the following:

- Things (dhamma), conceptions, thoughts, ideas
- Mind activities (citta)
- Feelings or sensations (vedana)
- Body or physical activities (kaya)

There are many kinds of meditation techniques that aim to develop attentiveness. Anapanasati or concentration on breathing is also a popular practice for mental and body development. A person has to be aware how the mind works and how thoughts disappear and appear at all times – if the mind is concentrated or distracted, filled with kindness or hatred, full of truth or deluded, and lustful or not. A person has to learn about the nature of their thoughts – from conception, suppression to destruction and so on.

Right Concentration – This last factor of mental discipline leads to recueillement or trance or the four stages of Dhyana, as follows:

- First stage – A person keeps the feelings of happiness, joy and other mental activities and discards skeptical doubt, restlessness, worry, languor, ill-will, unwholesome thoughts, and passionate desires.

- Second stage – A person keeps the feelings of happiness and joy while suppressing intellectual activities until the mind develops one-pointedness and tranquility.

- Third stage – A person keeps the disposition of happiness, but joy is discarded to get to the point of mindful equanimity.

- Fourth stage – Awareness and pure equanimity remain but all sensations, including sorrow, joy, and happiness are discarded.

The noble eightfold path is not to be used for sequential learning, but rather as the eight aspects of life which have to be integrated in your daily life. It creates an environment that will lead you further into finding the Buddhist path.

The path isn't religious in nature but more on the realization of one's completeness in terms of peace through intellectual, spiritual, and moral perfection, happiness, freedom, and utmost reality.

In Buddhism, it is meant to be used as a guideline to be considered, learned, contemplated on, and to be taken on when each step has been fully accepted to be a part of the life one person seeks to lead.

Buddhism does not teach its followers for blind faith, rather it asks people to promote the joys of learning and the process of self-discovery.

The five precepts were among Buddha's first teachings. He knew it would be challenging to apply these five precepts in all areas of life but will help a lot to ease a person's emotional stress and struggles. These precepts make a vital part of the noble eightfold path. In reciting the precepts, the target usually involves the following:

1. Never take lives, including insects.

2. Never steal nor get anything not given freely.

3. Never get involved in illicit sexual acts.

4. Never speak harshly, gossip and lies.

5. Never consume intoxicants that cloud the mind.

Chapter 3 - The Three Marks of Existence of Buddha

Everything that the Buddha taught his followers contained the three marks of existence or the three characteristics common in all his teachings. These three marks are anicca or impermanence, dukkha or suffering/dissatisfaction, and anatta or not-self. They apply to all things except for nirvana. Buddha said that in order to realize enlightenment, one has to appreciate and fully understand the three marks of existence. This concept is more emphasized in the Theravada school but is also taught in Mahayana school.

Anicca

Buddha always believed that everything changes. We should never think of anybody or anything as permanent. Even people's lives are not permanent. The moment that you forget the notion is when you feel hurt and stressed out.

Dukkha

Nothing is permanent, including emotions. You may feel satisfied with something, such as having a new car, eating a wonderful dish or spending quality time with friends, but the feeling won't last. For Buddha, life is dukkha, but it doesn't mean that it is always filled with unhappiness. What he meant was that ultimately, the feeling will pass, and you will realize that it is not enough to feel the same way for the rest of your life.

Anatta

Nothing is permanent, including the existing self inside each individual. There is no absolute identity. There is no "I" or "self". Having an illusion of a permanent self bind you to dissatisfaction and suffering. You do everything to protect your notion of "self" but by doing so, you develop certain cravings that lead to suffering, like what was told in the four noble truths.

By learning more about the teachings of Buddha, including the application of the eightfold path, you will develop less attachment to material and other impermanent things. Upon discovering the truths behind the three marks of existence, it will be easier to learn the important factors towards enlightenment. These factors are serenity and equanimity or the point when you can no longer be controlled by your likes and dislikes.

Chapter 4 - Karma and Zen in Buddhism

The Law of Karma

The term and concept of karma have been used in different religions in India before the time of Buddha. He interpreted the term as the intention or the cause of action. He formulated the doctrine, which is now considered as fundamental in Buddhism. One of the insights that Buddha learned on the night he was enlightened was about karmic conditioning and how it dictates the intentions behind the actions. This means that the intention was brought about by the actions and consequences of what they have done. On that night, Buddha was able to see his past lives and the actions he took that brought him to his enlightenment.

Buddha believed that karma is mutable even though it comes from the result of the karma you have accumulated from your past to present lives. Each day gives you an opportunity to change the negative into positive and to follow his teachings towards a better tomorrow.

For Buddhists, nothing in this world happens by accident. In one way or another, a person deserves whatever happens to them. The reasons may be traced either in their present life or past life. A person is responsible for his own misery and happiness. You create your fate, as well as your own heaven and hell.

Zen in Buddhism

Zen, formerly known as the Chan School, started during the Tang dynasty in China. It is a school of Mahayana Buddhism that later on branched out into different schools. Its formation is traced to dhyāna, and Indian practice that means meditation.

Zen focuses on understanding the true nature of things, meditation practice, and strict self-control. It promotes interaction with a qualified teacher and spiritual practice to achieve direct understanding. It veers away from emphasizing mere lessons about doctrine and sutras.

Dhyana or jhana refers to the practice that leads to the state of perfect awareness or equanimity. It is commonly called meditation, which trains the mind to disassociate from instant responses to the impressions of the senses. It was included in the pre-sectarian Buddhism's core practice, along with other practices leading to utmost detachment and mindfulness.

In Chinese Buddhism, dhyana incorporates different meditation techniques and important practices applied in the preparatory stage. The five main meditation techniques practiced in the process include the following:

- Contemplation on the Buddha
- Contemplation on the 12 links of pratītyasamutpāda

- Loving-kindness or maitrī meditation
- Mindfulness of the body's impurity or paṭikūlamanasikāra meditation
- Mindfulness of breathing or ānāpānasmṛti

The goal of this technique is to understand the dhyana and purify the mind and improve its focus. The five techniques are also referred to as the ways for pacifying or stilling the mind.

In Zen teachings, students are taught to focus and count their breaths to control their minds. They either count both inhalations and exhalation or, only one of the two. The process is repeated until the mind is calm. Breathing for this purpose is often diaphragmatic. It means that the breath must come from hara or under the navel.

Chapter 5 - Ethics and Other Vital Things To Understand in Buddhism

Buddhism encourages people to examine their words and actions if they are causing harm to others or themselves. Anything that causes harm should be avoided or else, such words or actions will cause the suffering of oneself and of others. The eightfold path or the path of practice of Buddha encompasses ways to live ethically.

By living ethically, your mind becomes lighter and more free, which makes it easier to see things clearly and focus. You'll find it hard to concentrate during meditation when you know that you have done something wrong or you've said a lie. This will be harder for you to find your way towards spiritual enlightenment.

How to Deal with Fear

In Buddhism, it is believed that fear is a mistake in perception. It is something that is rooted in the made-up images that took over your mind. You have to deal with your perceptions in order to deal with fear. Feeling this way also means that you are lacking love and have attention problems. Those who stay at the moment and live with love and compassion are less likely to feel fear.

The seeds of conflict, according to Buddhism, come from selfishness, envy, and bitterness. When you have these emotions and you lack love, you become susceptible and an open breeding ground to fear. You have to feel stronger to conquer your fears.

One source of fear is attachment, with polar opposites include spiritual and mental peace. You develop an attachment when you become too focused on attaining things and emotions. After getting what you want, the next thing you will feel is the fear of losing them. The more attached you become to these things, feelings, or people, the stronger the fear you'll feel about losing them. As your fear heightens, the more attached you become to the sources of the feeling.

To avoid or overcome fear, Buddhism teaches people to accept that everything is temporary. You have to feel detached and accept that you don't own anything or anyone, not even your life. All that you have now, including your life, is only temporary. It is better to stop trying having things to lessen the chances of feeling fear.

Another factor that plays a great role in developing fear is the habit of dwelling on committed mistakes. This action feeds anxiety and fear. Mistakes are normal in life. The only way you can get past them is by learning from your mistakes. If you don't learn from them, you will only risk the chance of committing the same mistakes over and over again.

The fundamental essence of fear, according to Buddhism, is dwelling too much on rejection toward suffering. Pain equates to your understanding of fear and suffering is how you handle it. Suffering is said to be optional while pain is bound to happen.

Pain becomes too powerful and causes fear when you don't handle it well. To avoid fear out of pain, you must not suffer from the emotion by learning to accept pain. Only then will pain lose its power and instead of feeling fear, you will try to understand where it came from and try to learn from it.

When you deal with fear, you also deal with suffering. Buddhism suggests to always focus on the present to deal with fear. This kind of attitude will keep your mind from overthinking and feeding yourself with unfounded fears.

Learning how to effectively deal with fear takes persistence and patience. Meditating often will help in speeding up the process.

Rebirth

According to the teachings of Buddhism, a person is reborn after death. The cycle of death and rebirth will go on until one reaches the point of nirvana. The concept of a person in Buddhism is composed of perceptions, feelings, and thoughts that constantly interact. The mental energy doesn't stop after the death of a person. It will only reenter and establish again in another body.

There are different Buddhist beliefs about how long it takes before the rebirth process. There are some teachings that say it takes 49 days while others say that it happens immediately after death.

Other Vital Things to Understand about Buddhism

What does emptiness mean to Buddhist practitioners?

The term, emptiness, comes from the Pali word – sunnata or sunyata in Sanskrit. The term was met with confusion at first since it connotes a negative feeling. Later on, the concept of emptiness was expanded on Heart Sutra, a famous Mahayana scripture. It states that everything is relative or empty. Nothing exists with any substantial reality – from the mind itself to the tiniest of particles on earth.

Is it important to believe in rebirth to be called a Buddhist?

Most Buddhists look into their lives in the context of rebirth. This doesn't mean that they believe in it, but they see each individual as part of a bigger story and a bigger world. Many western Buddhists wouldn't find it offensive even if you don't believe in the concept of rebirth. You are your own boss. You can do and believe whatever pleases you, but it wouldn't hurt to prepare just in case you experience getting reborn. This will even make you a better person, you have nothing to lose.

How important is faith in Buddhism?

Faith isn't encouraged in Buddhism. It doesn't promote any particular belief. Even Buddha didn't want his disciples to rely solely on his teachings. Faith means a personal experience in Buddhism. It means to trust or be confident on your journey towards enlightenment. In many Buddhist schools, faith is defined as taking refuge in the dharma or teachings of Buddha. Most of them share the commitment to the path while being guided by the wisdom and example of sangha, dharma, and Buddha.

Chapter 6 - Start Your Spiritual Path

Going to retreats is a good way to start your spiritual path. This will allow you to explore not only Buddhism but more about yourself. In the West, you'll find a lot of Buddhist retreat centers that include monasteries and dharma centers.

For those who don't have time, reading books and learning the ways to meditate in a similar way like the Buddhists is a good start. Once you are ready to explore and experience what it is like outside the books, you can try finding the nearest centers in your place. If you can allot time and money, you can also join retreats in exotic places or into the wilderness.

The good thing about joining retreats is that you'll have a company and most of you are beginners. You will all learn together the protocols, nature of the exercises, meditation and other teachings involved in the process.

When joining a Buddhist retreat, it is important to manage your expectations. Do not expect anything luxurious. This is far from a vacation or a day at the spa. You will learn how to live like Buddha – simple and free from the riches. Certain facilities require the sharing of bathrooms. There are monasteries that expect the participants to help with the chores during their stay. Sleeping isn't a luxury either since monks will walk in before dawn with clanging bells to start a chanting program or an early meditation.

It is also likely that you'll be required to participate in Buddhist rituals. This is something that doesn't sit well on many postmodern westerners who don't approve of chanting unfamiliar words or paying homage to golden Buddha figures.

Despite certain setbacks, a Buddhist retreat for beginners is a once in a lifetime spiritual experience and a personal adventure. It will open your eyes to reality as you've never seen before. It will help you in finding greater spiritual intensity and depth.

It is not easy to find a good Buddhist retreat. You have to be on the lookout of the real ones that will not take advantage of you. You can try finding good retreat centers at directories online or known Buddhist publications.

If you want an authentic Buddhist experience, research about the centers you're interested in. There are certain centers, which advertise that they are Buddhist, but actually, they are not. Ask about the qualifications of the teacher who will conduct the retreat. An authentic one will be honest in telling you all about their Buddhism background and education.

A real Buddhist retreat place offers well-established practices. You can also opt to join centers that offer a fusion of practices and activities. They will be upfront about what they have to offer and explain the Buddhism aspects and the other practices involved in the retreat.

A beginner should always start in a beginner's retreat. You will need the experience before you can join the more intensive rituals offered at many dharma centers. Getting into an advanced retreat center without prior experience will make it difficult for you to understand the protocols and rituals. You might end up having a bad experience despite getting into an authentic retreat center.

How to Become a Buddhist Monk?

You can become a monk as long as you have a pure intent of becoming one. You have to be sincere in learning about the practice and all the Buddha's teachings.

Learning

1. You must first have the interest before committing yourself to the process. Understand the basic concept of Buddhism and familiarize yourself with the teachings of Buddha. You can begin by reading books and researching. You can then enroll yourself in classes headed by ordained Buddhist monks. The most basic concepts you need to learn at the start include the following:

    - The Eightfold Path
    - The Four Noble truths

2. Look for a sangha or temple that practices Buddhism. You'll find one anywhere in the world you are since the religion is practiced worldwide. Join and be part of the community. You have to commit your time to it. Do not give yourself a deadline when you enter the temple. This will serve as a test if this is the right path for you. You will learn a lot from the process but how long you would last will depend on your realizations. You can prematurely leave the temple if you can't see yourself following the same practices that Buddhists do for the rest of your life. You can also stay for weeks, months, or even years before deciding whether you want to adapt to the practice or not.

While in the temple, be an active participant as much as possible. The activities and teachings depend on the sangha you've enrolled yourself into. There are sanghas that focus on helping people grow in their faith, as well as ones that offer introductory courses about the religion. The Buddhist communities may vary. Others may have adapted to the changing times while some have stuck their teachings to traditional Buddhism. Your goal is to find the community that is most appealing and suited to your personality and beliefs.

You can try visiting various temples before choosing which one to join. This will give you a better idea of their similarities and differences.

3. You will need a mentor. In order to become a monk, you will need a spiritual guide or mentor. He will teach you and guide you throughout the process. You will learn a lot from your mentor – a deeper look into the religion, a step-by-step guide to fulfill your goal and understanding what to expect once you become a monk.

It will be easier to find a mentor once you have joined a temple. They will often invite Buddhist leaders to share their experiences and the teachings of Buddha. You can ask about them and choose which one you will approach to become your mentor.

Preparation

1. Commit your time in meditating as you prepare yourself for the monastic life. A Buddhist monk meditates every day. They are consciously doing it to change how their minds work. It is essential to commit most of your time meditating when you live in an abbey. It's not easy but it can be done through practice.

There are many kinds of meditation you can practice in Buddhism. It can include focusing on postures, a meditation on the Lamrim, transformation, and breathing. You can begin doing the practice twice a day for at least five minutes each session. You can gradually increase the time you spend in the process until you can last 15 minutes per session twice a day. You will learn from your mentor that monks spend hours in meditating.

2. You'll be required to follow the code of conduct called Vinaya to become a Buddhist monk. This means that you'll need to support yourself for up to three years. It is stipulated in the Vinaya that nuns and Buddhist monks can't work a normal day job to earn a living.. In certain cases, the abbey you're situated in will give your basic needs but in most cases, you need to have sufficient savings to support yourself.

3. You have to get used to a life without luxury. As a monk, you only need to possess what you need and nothing else. You will live as a mendicant without worldly possession. You'll get supplies of your basic needs – sundries, clothing, and other things you'll need from day to day. You cannot have anything that could evoke possessiveness, envy, or greed. You will lead a simple life.

4. It is important to discuss the decision with your family and let them understand the changes that will happen once you become a monk. You'll be devoted to your advocacy to help those in need and your Buddhist community will become your new family. You'll have very limited interaction with your family.

There are certain monasteries who only accept single people without strong relationship ties. There are others that don't allow married candidates to become monks. They prefer people who can devote themselves to the religion without any distractions, such as relationships and strong ties outside of the monastery.

5. Practice chastity before committing yourself to become a monk. Monks are required to take a vow of chastity. They can't get involved in any kind of sexual behavior. There are even instances when female and male monks are prohibited to talk to one another about topics not related to Buddhism. This is done to conserve energy and put it to matters considered more important than the self.

6. Talk to your mentor about the kinds of commitment you can choose from before deciding on the matter. There are certain traditions that will require ordination for several months or years. There are other traditions that require a lifelong commitment to the practice after getting ordained.

For example, many men in Tibet complete ordinations of two to three months to gain a clearer perspective about their spirituality before pursuing their careers or getting married. If you are unsure about yourself but still want to try the life of a monk, you can try the shorter span of ordination. If you liked it, then you can join the lifelong ordination or if not, you still have time to leave and pursue the other things your heart desires.

Ordination

1. When you have decided that you really want to pursue the life of a monk, you have to train at an abbey. You have to meet the requirements and rules set by the specific abbey you're in to be obtained. In some cases, you will need a referral from an elder to appoint you as a candidate to become a monk.

2. The ordination can only be done by an ordained monk. You have to attend the ceremony wherein the monk will hand to you the Five Precepts and three Jewels. You will also be given a Buddhist name.

3. The one who ordained you will teach you about what to do next. You'll be briefed about the rules and what to expect on the monastery you'll be part of.

4. You will take the Bodhisattva Vows, which focus on searching for enlightenment, working for the good of all human beings and doing compassionate action. You will become a Bodhisattva or a person whose life is devoted to Buddhist practice. You have to recite the vows regularly. They serve as a reminder of what you're

striving for and to your commitment to a selfless service throughout your life.

Chapter 7 – Training The Mind With Meditation

Many people's idea of meditation is that of a Tibetan monk peacefully sitting on a mountaintop or a yogic practitioner with eyes closed and chanting the sound of "Om" in a candlelit room.

There are many ways to meditate and it could mean different things to different people. The clear idea here is that it offers many health benefits and can be done by anyone.

Untrained minds are hard to satisfy. You will constantly feel the longing to attain more even when your ego tells you to stop. Meditation helps in making you realize that you are different from your ego, your personality or your mind.

Behind the physical qualities, you are composed of a limitless ocean of pure bliss. Once you realize this truth, it will be easier to reach your highest potential and experience true contentment and joy.

Dealing with Stress

You will find it hard to meditate if you are often stressed or get easily frustrated over petty reasons. Learn how to deal with stress first by doing the proven techniques to get rid of it.

1. Imagine yourself as a child without too many things to worry about. Let your mind go on a trip down the memory lane. Try to remember as many happy memories as you can when you were little. Observe how your feelings become lighter as you remember those fond memories.

2. Recall how your parents dealt with your naughtiness and how they were able to control their temper a lot of times when you were young. Go back to the times when you did something untoward. Imagine how your parents handled the situation with calmness. You can use these memories to soothe your temper and control your anger whenever needed.

3. Free yourself from all gadgets while at home, especially when you are not expecting calls or messages from work. Instead of watching TV or using the computer, play soothing music, sit back, relax, and enjoy the

sound. If you want, you can turn off the music and learn how to enjoy the silence for silence is good.

4. Sleep. Your physical body may already be too tired from everything you've done. It may be the cause of your grumpiness and the heaviness you are feeling inside. Rest but don't oversleep. Oversleeping will only worsen your feelings of fatigue.

    If you have difficulty sleeping and you badly needed to rest, go in your room, and set the temperature the way you like it. Play some soothing music, diffuse some relaxing essential oils, and wear your most comfortable clothes. Forget about your worries as you dive into your bed to give your mind and body enough time to rest and recharge.

5. Get comfortable and be your natural self when at home. Look and act silly if you must. Everybody needs this kind of feeling every once in a while, to be at a place where you don't have to prove yourself. Enjoy yourself when you're at home and leave all your worries in the office or school. You have to give this time to yourself to feel better and be prepared for the next busy days.

6. Many people find their kitchens the most relaxing spot at home. Cook or bake and indulge in the kinds of activities you enjoy. You will feel lighter in the process

and happier as well. You can choose not to do anything in the kitchen but to smell the scents of your favorite ingredients. No matter what you do, take your time, and enjoy the process. See things as if you're seeing them for the first time as you explore your most favorite spot at home.

7. Clean. Cleaning can help in relieving stress, especially for people who can't stand anything dirty and in disorder. You can set a date when you will do a complete makeover of your home. Do it at times when you are experiencing too much stress. The result of the activity – a cleaner and more organized home, will make you feel lighter and relieve your stress as well.

    You can also spend the first 10 to 15 minutes of your day in tidying up your home. This is considered as an exercise, which can help in boosting your mood and energy.

8. Turn your home into a sanctuary. Always remind yourself that this is your place and you can do anything you want as long as it pleases you. Turn your home into the kind of place you will look forward coming to after spending a stressful day at work. Paint the house with your favorite color or shades that help in calming the nerves, such as white or green. Display images, figurines or toys that make you feel happy. Put new

curtains and diffuse relaxing scents whenever you're at home. The scent will linger inside when you go out and welcome you with its invigorating effect when you go back.

Other Effective Ways to Get Rid of Stress

There are days when you get hit by too much stress that you find it hard to focus, concentrate, and meditate. You can't control the nagging voice inside your head. There are too many distractions and you're getting defeated by them. When you find yourself in the situation, here are some of the most effective ways to deal with too much stress:

1. Laugh more often

    When you are feeling weary due to stress, laugh at the situation and laugh at yourself. Laugh hard and give it your all. Try to remember a funny situation or a joke you heard that made you laugh so hard. You can also watch your favorite funny video clips. Even without reason, you can force yourself to laugh. It may seem unnatural at first but as you go on laughing, you will start to find something amusing about the process and the laughter will come out naturally. This is a good exercise in relieving stress. Laughing relaxes your muscles and helps in releasing endorphins in the brain.

2. Listen to nature

This is a good way to remind yourself that there is a bigger world you are a part of. The circumstances may not be working in your favor at the moment, but this phase will pass. For now, you have to calm your nerves to pacify the mind and think clearly. You can do this indoors or outdoors. If you are in the office, excuse yourself for a while, go out, sit on a bench and close your eyes. Listen intently to nature sounds, like the animals nearby and the whistling of air. Indoors, you can listen to a seashell and imagine that you are in a paradise for that brief moment.

You can also put a miniature fountain at your desk and listen to the sounds as you try to relax, sit back and allow yourself to feel comfortable and soothed.

If you are technologically savvy, you can download some apps you can use for this kind of activity. There are apps with nature sounds you can use to help relax your mind and body.

3. Smell your favorite essential oils.

   There is a part of the brain responsible for governing your memory and emotions. Near this area is the part that processes scents. The latter can induce good emotions and help in calming your mind.

A study published in 2008 proved that the use of essential oils in nurses who work in intensive care units helped in alleviating and managing their tension and stress. You can dab a small amount of oil with your favorite scent in your clothes or skin. You can also use a diffuser to allow all the people in the room to benefit from its scent. The essential oils known to relieve stress include lavender, ylang-ylang, and peppermint.

4. Perform breathing exercises. A minute of this exercise is enough to ease the tension inside of you. Close your eyes, breathe deeply and let your mind focus on your breathing. Feel your body when you breathe. You will feel better when you go back to the current moment. You will also notice that your mood is lighter and your outlook in life clearer.

5. Give yourself a brief massage. The stress triangle in the body is found at the neck and shoulders. Stop what you're doing when you're stressed out. Try to relax as you massage your neck and shoulders. Focus on how your hands and fingers are moving and how the massage alleviates your tiredness and stress. Focus the massage on your stress triangle.

6. Dance. This is a good form of exercise as it helps in releasing and pumping up the endorphins in your system. Put on your earphones and play a tune. Let

your body dance to the beat as if no one's watching. Continue even when there are people around. This will make you feel better and happier.

Getting Started with Seated Meditation

If you want to learn how to meditate, you can start by following these steps:

1. Find the perfect spot where you can meditate undisturbed. It can be indoors or outdoors, as long as it is peaceful and quiet. Make sure that the space can give you a total solitude during the process. Clean the spot and keep it neat. It will be hard to focus in a cluttered space. Set the mood and ambiance by lighting a candle but you can skip this part if you are not fond of its smell. Place anything in your chosen spot that will make it easier for you to get "in the zone," such as music or incense.

2. It will take time to get used to the process. As much as possible, minimize the possible distractions when you begin. The biggest distraction will be your own mind. No matter what thoughts it comes up with, keep your focus and try to go back to meditating. Set a goal on what you want to achieve, including how long you intend the session to last. You can start the practice

with 20 minutes per session. You can gradually add time through the days and as you get more used to it.

3. Keep proper posture all the time while meditating and make sure that you are comfortable with it. Sitting properly will minimize the discomfort and pain while proper posture helps you breathe deeper and easier.

   You can choose to sit however you like - with a cushion or without, on a chair or on the floor. You can also opt to stand if you'll find it more comfortable. No matter how you position yourself, never lose your balance, never lean on anything and never slouch. Adjust your position if you feel any kind of pain. As to constantly meditate, you will find the best and appropriate position for you.

4. Focus on your breathing - how the air flows in and out of your system, your belly getting filled and empty and upward and downward motion of your chest. Breathe slow but not deliberately. Feel the ebb, flow, and rhythm of the process.

5. Be aware of yourself and all the areas of your body. Learn how to recognize where the discomfort or tension is coming from. There are certain parts of the body where stress usually gets "stored", such as the face, neck, back, shoulders, and legs.

You have to relax as you meditate and the best way to do this is by getting rid of the tension and stress. Imagine the tension coming out of your system as you breathe out until you have released all the tension and you finally feel at ease.

Refining Your Meditation Practice

After learning the basics, you can focus on training your mind. Concentrate on how to reach true happiness, compassion, inner peace, and patience.

Here are the steps to follow to improve your concentration while meditating:

1. Practice mindfulness. Concentration and mindfulness are referred to as the two wings of meditation in Buddhism. They are opposite but work together like wings. Mindfulness remains open and relaxed at times when concentration is one-pointed. Mindfulness becomes expansive while concentration is focused.

   At this point, you have to learn how to grow and expand your awareness. Feel your breath as air is distributed all over your system, senses, emotions, thoughts, and mind. Whenever something comes to mind, accept it and release so that you can go back in opening and freeing your awareness.

Observe everything present in the moment but do not grasp anything all at once Learn how to recognize things, emotions, and thoughts and let them go. As you practice meditation, it will be easier to rest, stay peaceful, and come to this state.

2. Improve your mental discipline through control and focus. You have to learn how to focus your attention. This aspect of meditation seems simple but it's actually one of the most difficult to control.

You can begin by choosing one thing as the object you'll focus on. It can be your breath, the flame of a lit candle or a mantra. Hold your attention to your focus. Take a mental note of whatever distracted you as you're doing the process.

Distractions come in many forms - a random thought or feeling, noise or an itch. As you set aside the distraction, bring back your attention to your focus.

It is normal to find this activity hard in the beginning. There will be times when you'll get distracted not only by things or your thoughts but also by certain emotions, such as boredom and frustration. Just hold on to the practice and keep on doing it. You will get better at it in time.

Through continued practice, your mind will find it easier to become more steady. You'll be able to allow distractions and thoughts fade from sight without affecting you. The object of your focus becomes a calm refuge, a sanctuary or an island that you can go back into whenever you need healing.

3. You don't silence your mind when you meditate, contrary to popular belief. It is not your enemy, but it can be a powerful tool and your friend with the right training and attitude.

   When you pay attention, you will realize the same thought pattern repeating in your mind as you practice mindfulness or concentration. The recurring thoughts may be telling you something. They may be fantasies, dreams or memories that exist to teach you. They will serve as the keys to open any mental blockage, which includes subconscious thinking that refrains you from reaching your full potential, fears, and deeply held beliefs.

   Just let the thought come in and do not fight them. Befriend your thoughts instead, including the unpleasant ones. Invite all the learnings you've gotten from the thoughts as you find out more about your inner workings - why are you like that and why do love doing the things you love to do. Your goal is to make the unconscious conscious. You can achieve this by bringing into the light the darkest and deepest parts of your mind.

4. As you cultivate pure awareness through meditation, you have to practice non-judgment. Learn not to judge your thoughts whether they are right or wrong and good or bad. Let all the feelings, memories, and thoughts flow through your awareness. Do not label them but merely observe what is happening. Having bad thoughts don't mean that you are a bad person, same as having good thoughts make you a good person.

   Observe your fantasies and memories as they unfold and listen to your thoughts. Your mind doesn't define who you are.

5. Do not identify yourself with the voice in your head – the voice that constantly plans, worry, remember, label, judge, and repeat thoughts over and over again. You are not your personality, mind, and ego. They are all lies that you can get yourself freed from through meditation. The process empowers the truth of what and who you really are. You can make that happen by first, stopping from identifying yourself from your fearful ego.

You are not required to silence your ego. That would be impossible. You simply have to shift your personality to become an observer and spectator. Whatever you are thinking are only thoughts. Thinking happens and you don't have anything to do with it.

When you reach the point of realization and successfully shifted your personality, you will feel what it's like to be free. You will feel lighter as if a heavy burden has been lifted off your life. The thoughts in your head must never limit who you are and your full potential. Always remember that you are a pure and vast ocean of awareness that becomes a witness to everything inside and outside of you. You can do whatever you want because you are free.

6. Meditation allows you to uncover recurring thought patterns, such as limiting beliefs, judgments, and fears. The process helps you understand what the rest of the world expects from you and most important of all, develop your basic concept of who you really are. Once you allow meditation to transform you, it will shape your character and how you relate to other people, your behavior and all aspects of your life.

The process leads to the point of understanding that most of your thoughts aren't true and they only form barriers and try to limit you. Let go of these limiting thoughts and beliefs.

7. The most difficult skill you have to develop as you meditate is the art of letting go or surrendering. You have to let go of your so-called self, get rid of who you thought you are and realize the limitless potentials and opportunities.

Every time you go to your sacred place to meditate, you have to be open and aware. Give yourself fully to the experience, the stillness, and silence.

It will be easier through time. Make sure that you never compare your progress to others. You are unique and this is a good way to realize what kind of unique you are.

Chapter 8 - Different Kinds of Meditation

Metta Meditation

This type of meditation helps its practitioners develop compassion, which is one of the main goals of Buddhism. This is popular, universal, and accessible to everybody.

The word, Meta, is a term with no literal English translation but it conveys fellowship, compassion, goodwill, benevolence, non-violence, friendliness, and warmth. The word comes from ancient Pali or a language from the most ancient scriptures of Buddhism. To give it an English translation, the term loving-kindness was made.

The practice and philosophy of this kind of meditation can be rooted in the Hymn of Universal Love - the Karaniya Metta Sutta of Buddha. Through this Hymn of Universal Love, Buddha taught his disciples proper contemplation and development of compassion and universal love to achieve spiritual perfection and liberation.

In order to perform this kind of meditation properly, you must first understand what compassion is all about. Compassion, while having a meaning close to empathy, differs from the latter. Empathy allows you to feel other's suffering as if you are the one going through it. While it can be said that compassion is an extension of empathy, it doesn't end to feeling the other person's suffering. Empathy makes you feel stuck. It is draining, stressful and not helpful to you or the person who is going through something.

When you take empathy to the next level, that's when you will feel compassion. At this point, you will identify with the sufferer and not merely relate to how they are feeling. You'd have a desire of taking off their baggage and you will feel love and warmth towards them.

According to studies, compassion and empathy stimulate different networks in the brain. The positive feelings, such as kindness, love, connection, and warmth are associated with networks with underlying compassion. Negative emotions, on the other hand, are associated with networks that underlying empathy.

Compassion puts the feeling of empathy to good use. It is proactive because you will realize that you are also helping yourself as you help others.

Compassion has numerous benefits according to research. They include the following:

- Alleviates chronic pain
- Alleviates migraine
- Alleviates signs of aging
- Alleviates stress
- Prompts positive changes in the brain

Compassion is also beneficial to emotional and mental wellbeing:

- Boosts positive emotions
- Heals self-criticism
- Improves mood and emotions
- Boosts emotional intelligence
- Helps in treating mental disorders, such as schizophrenia and PTSD
- Reduces the symptoms of depression

Some of its social benefits include the following:

- It helps you become more cooperative and helpful
- Boosts your social connection
- Helps in dealing with bias and prejudices

Here are the steps on how to practice Metta or Loving-Kindness Meditation

1. Find your sacred place and position yourself comfortably. Keep your back relaxed and straight without feeling any pain.

2. Practice a simple breathing meditation for the first few minutes. Inhale deeply as you scan your system for any tension, pain, and stress. Exhale slowly while you release the negative feelings with each exhalation. Keep focused on your breathing while adjusting your position whenever needed. As you go through the breathing exercises, allow yourself to go deeper until you reach the state of total relaxation.

3. Once the body is completely relaxed and your mind is at peace, chant words that will make you feel calmer. The chant has to revolve around yourself like these:

> *"May I be joyful, peaceful, and safe."*

> *"May I discover the real me."*

> *"May I be free from pain and suffering."*

You must first cultivate loving-kindness to yourself because you can only give love and compassion to others if you love and feel compassionate about yourself. Chant the words while feeling happy, at peace, free, and smiling. Imagine that you are in a perfect world where happiness is everywhere, without danger or fear.

As you recite the words, imagine a vision of complete serenity. Feel the love in your core and accept the feeling and the warmth it brings. Accept who you are, love that person, forgive and be kind to yourself. Stay in this state for 2 to 3 minutes.

4. You will now direct the loving-kindness to other people. Think about the closest or those in your inner circle. You will think of them one by one. The chant can be similar with the first one but this time, you'll address your chants to each of your loved one like:

> *"May you be joyful, peaceful, and safe."*

"May you discover the real you."

"May you be free from pain and suffering."

Imagine your loved one being free, happy, and well as you perform the chant. You will visualize them overcoming problems and challenges. Imagine them discovering the divine and infinite being.

5. You will chant the same thing as what you said in the previous step but this time, you'll think about other people who don't belong in your inner circle. They can be anyone you can think of – a person you met on the street or at the mall, your neighbor or co-worker. Relax the chant whole thinking of the person who first come to your mind. Think about them while wishing for their well-being. Be sincere with your desire for them to attain spiritual freedom, healthy body, and peaceful mind.

6. At this point, you will think of a person or people who have hurt or caused you pain. You will recite the same chant in steps 4 to 5 while thinking about each of them. Call them out and silently chant the phrases. You will then observe how you feel as you perform the chant. You have to be aware if you are feeling any resistance or if feels like you are still holding resentment, pain, anger, and frustration towards them. You can move forward to the next step if you feel like you have already forgiven what they have done. If not, you will need to

work on forgiving these people until can recite the chants like you mean them

7. You will now include all living things in your chant. Using the same chant in steps 4 to 6, you will recite them while thinking about all living things in the universe, including animals, plants, and humans. As you say the chant, imagine your mind and heart like a fully bloomed lotus flower. Visualize all living things on earth and all the universe as part of an infinite whole. Keep the vision until it feels real.

You can perform this kind of meditation twice a day at about 20 minutes each per session.

Moving Meditation

Everybody can meditate, even those who find it hard to sit still, such as people diagnosed with ADHD or ADD. You can try any of the following alternatives to the most common sitting meditation:

1. Mindful Walking

This walking meditation popularized by Buddhist monk Thich Nhat Hanh is done by simply walking while working on your focus and attention. This is best done outdoors. As you walk, focus on your breathing and on your every step. Keep your attention to your senses, breath, body, and whatever is happening at the moment. Relax as you walk. You can do this anytime and anywhere. You can practice this kind of meditation as you walk to or from home.

2. Painting or drawing

Bring out the artist in you and indulge on your talent. Art can heal. Most artists consider their art as sacred and more than a craft. The process of doing the art will get you in the zone, especially if it is your passion. In the zone means that you'll enter into the state of surrender and mindfulness. Painting and writing have long been considered as forms of meditation in the far East. They help them achieve peace, mindfulness and give them the feeling of freedom and spontaneity.

You don't need to be good to start with this form of meditation. Relax, loosen up, try something new and play with your imagination. Choose what you will use – crayons, paints or pen and choose space. This space has to be peaceful and where you can be left alone while seeking for a much-needed silence. This space must inspire you to work on your art while keeping your focus. Place all the materials you'll need within reach.

Decide on what you will draw or paint. It can be anything – an abstract, landscape, shapes, fruit or flower. Enjoy the process and let your medium go wherever it wants to go and create whatever they whatever it wants to create. Do not mind the end product. You don't have to show it to anyone, and it doesn't need to be perfect. Release your worries and focus on having fun.

3. Tai Chi

It comes from the term, *tai chi chuan*, which means supreme ultimate force. The exercise aims to balance and enhance the body's energy flow – the chi or qi or the cosmic life force. The practice involves a series of easy movements mostly inspired by nature. Many of the motions done in Tai Chi are similar to martial arts. You will focus on your breathing as you perform deliberate, gentle, and slow movements. You will continue with the practice until you become balanced, centered, and calm.

You will challenge yourself with more difficult movements as you get used to the practice. In time, you will also learn surrender to the flow of energy and still your mind. The practice will make you forget the difference between active and passive, motion and stillness, the rest of the universe and yourself. When you reach that point, you will realize that you are the ultimate supreme force. You are the Chi.

3. Martial Arts

This is preferred by those who aren't used to doing the gentle movements of Tai Chi and yoga. Martial arts have the elements of engaged and active meditation. You can train your mind as you train your body during practice. There are many forms of martial arts that you can practice, such as kickboxing, karate, taekwondo, aikido and many more.

Choose what you want to practice and prepare a space where you will do it. Make sure that when you decide to start on the practice, you will dedicate the time in achieving mastery not only of the skills and movements but also of your self, life, and mind. While at it, keep your attention to your body and breathing. Let yourself get lost and absorbed in the movements.

4. Dancing, chanting, or singing

You don't need props or instruments to start meditating. You can use your voice and body. You can allow yourself to get lost in the melody or rhythm. Sing and dance your heart out. Have fun and without realizing, you'll eventually get into a meditative state of surrender, mindfulness, and relaxation.

To perform this kind of meditation, listen to your heart and do whatever feels right at the moment. You can dance along with your favorite tune or sing along with relaxing music, such as Gregorian chants or the traditional Indian kirtans. Let go and lose yourself in the moment.

5. Running

Most runners will tell you that the activity can be more than an exercise. It helps you reach the state called the runner's high or the meditative state while in motion. At this state, you'll feel in the moment, intensely alive and free from inner turmoil and mental chatter.

First, you have to decide that you'll do it and commit that you'll run the same time every day. This time will be your sacred time. You can do this anywhere you want – in the backyard, park, beach or road. Like the other forms of meditation, focus on your breathing. Keep your attention to the rhythm created by your feet while in motion. Feel the air as it moves past or along your body.

Be aware of your surroundings – the sunrise or sunset, the trees, other people, the gushing wind, the smell of the grass. Imbibe the moment and experience the present. The experience will make you feel light and happy, emotions that you'll look forward to each time that you have to do the activity again.

6. Yoga (Asanas)

Yoga is more than the physical poses required during the practice. It is comprised of different meditative practices, such as breathing exercises, self-inquiry, meditation and many more, which aim to help you reach the point of being one with God.

Chapter 9 - Cultivating Mindfulness

Mindfulness is an important concept in meditation practices and Buddhism. It refers to the act of paying close attention to the "now" or whatever's happening at the moment without being biased, without labels and judgment. It is pure awareness that happens before your mind works by doing cognitive tasks and thinking.

To practice mindfulness, you have to observe everything around you without overthinking or over-analyzing what you see. It is normal for judgments and unrelated thoughts to come up during the process. When this happens, try to stay calm as you focus your observation on what you're thinking.

When you have gotten into the state of pure awareness, you will find it easier to see things as they are. Everything becomes interesting, music sound better, food tastes better, and you'll see goodness in people. You will see life in variety, full of richness and color. You will let go of the filter that used to blur your vision and understanding of the world around you. You will also develop sharper senses and a disposition free from destructive thought patterns that lead to illnesses, anxiety, and depression.

You don't need to spend your whole life meditating to get into this state. You also don't have to be a Buddhist to experience the state of pure awareness.

Here are some of the activities and exercises you can do each day to make it easier for you to attain mindfulness that will last from day till night.

1. Start each day by waking up mindfully.

This will set the mood for the rest of your day. The moment you open your eyes, focus your awareness of the present moment – where you are, what you are doing, how you are feeling. Observe how you fee and what you sense. Do this first thing in the morning before getting up and before reaching your alarm clock.

Be aware of everything – every sound, smell, feeling, and more. Listen to the sounds coming from outside of the window, the noise created by your fan or cooler, the ringing of your alarm. Focus on your body and feel if there is any tension or if your eyelids feel heavy. Gently stretch your muscles as you observe the subtle sensations you feel as you become more awake. Observe but do not make judgments or any mental notes.

2. Practice mindfulness when you're taking a shower. As much as possible, teach your mind to observe without making a judgment. In the shower, observe all the things around you. As you begin with the process, run your hands to the water and feel its temperature. Look closely and observe how the water touches and slips through your form. Be observant of the feel

and smell of your shampoo, conditioner, soap, lotion, body wash, and all other products you'll use in the shower.

Smell the towel or roe and feel its texture as it rubs against your skin and hair. Observe the differences in the feeling of being dry and wet. Observe the toothpaste as you put some to your toothbrush. Be mindful of its taste and how the bristles of the toothbrush feel once inside your mouth. Avoid talking if you can and make sure that you are aware of the moment throughout the process.

3. Practice mindful eating.

Practice mindfulness at the first meal you'll have in the day, your breakfast. When in the kitchen, observe your body and hear what it says. Listen to its cravings or what does it want to have for breakfast. Observe every step and every movement you do as you prepare your meal to the moment that you have placed it on the table. As you eat, focus on your food and your body. Once your food is inside your mouth, chew it slowly. Let the flavor linger in your mouth as you pause in between. Feel the texture of the food and how it moves to your throat and belly. You must also be aware when your body is telling you that you're full.

4. Observe your habits

At times when you are not in a rush, try to observe the most common things you do each day and how you do them.

Observe each step of the activities you do almost every day. Start upon waking up. Observe what you usually do when you get out of bed. Be aware of what your body prefers doing and how you feel in each task. Observe each step of the task. Focus on the things that you could have skipped so you can spend time doing other useful chores. This exercise will not only help in practicing mindfulness but will also prompt you to become aware and give you an opportunity to wake up.

5. Practice mindfulness whenever you find yourself waiting

When your mind is busy, you tend to get easily frustrated when things slow down. If you find yourself waiting due for different reasons – traffic, long lines, the bus failed to show up, your date is late, and so on, use the waiting time to practice mindfulness instead of getting angry. Instead of thinking negatively about your situation, observe and practice mindfulness. While waiting, try to close your eyes, inhale, and relax.

Focus your awareness to your system and how you are feeling. Feel the emotion, anxiety, stress or tension. Breathe deeply and let go of the negative emotions and thoughts. Let them all go. The situation won't get light by getting angry or feeling tensed. You won't get to your destination or your date won't show up the moment you get angry. Relax and focus at what's happening at the moment. Whenever you are left to wait, make sure that you don't get mad. Instead, focus on the present, be mindful, and be aware.

6. Practice mindful driving

Consider your time at the car as your "me" time. From the point where you came from to your destination, you have to be aware of everything that has transpired – your car's temperature, the music playing, the sounds you hear, people and vehicles on the street. You have to focus on how you are driving and on the road ahead.

The next day, turn off the music and drive in silence. Refrain from talking or having other distractions. Bring your focus on the road. What do you see on the road and how do you feel. As you look closely, bring the attention of your senses on your feet and hands and what they are doing while you are driving. Focus on the sounds you hear, like the hum of the engine or the wind outside. Do not get distracted by your own thoughts. Let them be. Breathe deeply and bring back your attention to the very moment in the present.

7. Give yourself time to unwind

Upon coming home after a day at work or school, do not go straight on the couch or look for something to eat. Sit somewhere peaceful and spend a few minutes doing nothing but unwinding and relaxing. Be at the moment. Focus on what happened to your day and how it made you feel. Process any frustration, anger or tiredness. Keep on resting until you feel calmer. Make sure that you leave all negative feelings at this state. When you go back to usual, you'll feel calmer, happier, and rested.

8. Practice active listening

Give your loved ones or friends your undivided attention. Instead of tuning them out, try to actively listen to what they are saying. Concentrate on listening to them and do not compose your response in your head. This will hone your mindfulness and nurture your relationships as well. It gives you a chance to connect and be intimate with someone you care for.

Chapter 10 – Yoga and Buddhism

Yoga is not a religious system but is sometimes performed as part of certain religious practices. This practice has certain similarities to Buddhism. For one, they both aim to achieve enlightenment through the development of insightful wisdom and intuitive skills.

Buddha was also a serious practitioner of yoga and yogic arts. He sought an experiential understanding of the practice and he was also knowledgeable about the Vedantic philosophy. Yoga and Buddhism have the same core teaching, which is compassion. Both practices also recognize that freedom from a dualistic mindset leads to enlightenment. One type of yoga, Krishna, focuses on teaching the essence of equanimity of mind.

Buddha has expressed many times during his lifetime that one will only achieve the real meaning of freedom when they are free from their preferences and wants. Wanting something and not getting it will only lead to sadness and disappointment.

According to the yoga sutras of Patanjali, yoga is achieved when you can no longer identify the wavering of your mind. Once the state is achieved, you will experience Samadhi or identity with self that equates to ecstasy, bliss, and happiness. It also states that good karma comes from the practice of non-harming of others, also called ahimsa.

The yogic text Astavakra Samhita believes that a person will become whatever he thinks. A person eventually becomes eternal when he identifies with something that is eternal. He will be bound if that's how he thinks himself to be and free if he thinks himself as free.

Buddhism and yoga encourage people to be compassionate and kind toward other beings because everything that you do – action, word or thought, will eventually come back to you. They are both geared in achieving enlightenment or the state when a person realizes the totality of Oneness of Being. In order to achieve Oneness, you have to completely remove otherness. Oneness, in Buddhism, is referred to as the emptiness of form. Since otherness is considered as an obstacle, you have to make it disappear through compassion or one's ability to deeply see themselves in other people.

Another similarity between yoga and Buddhism is the recognition that suffering exists, but it is possible to free yourself from it. Both teachings utilize the meditation technique for the mind to go beyond hindrances and fluctuations. Yogis refer to the state as absolute self while it is referred to as emptiness in Buddhism.

Despite the similarities, the two practices also have various differences. Buddhism doesn't believe that God or a fundamental self exist. For Buddhists, these ideas were only created by the mind. The illusion of the self and creation of life were explained through conditioning and karma. For them, one's self is not something enduring but only a fleeting feeling or thought.

Yoga practitioners, on the other hand, believe in the existence of God and Atman or an Inner Self. The latter refers to one's soul or authentic self and the true nature of a person's consciousness. For them, God is not only the creator of the universe but also its preserver and destroyer. In order to gain self-realization in a yoga practice, you have to surrender yourself to God and have total faith in the Atman. In yoga, Atman is different from Ahamkara or ego. Both Buddhism and yoga are meditative practices in the search for higher consciousness.

Beginners Guide to Yoga

In order to benefit from yoga and use the practice to meditate and achieve enlightenment, you have to do it properly. Yoga can be done alone. You can follow a guide and perform the sequences on your own but is recommended to get a trainer or join a yoga class, especially in the beginning. You will need help not only with the movements and breathing but also on how to stay focused all throughout the process.

Different Styles of Yoga

It is important to acquaint yourself with the different styles of yoga to make it easier for you to find an instructor or yoga class. If you have an existing medical condition, make sure to open it up first to your instructor so that they can adjust the movements and pace depending on the state of your health.

Here are some of the most popular styles of yoga that you can choose from:

1. Bikram Yoga

Yoga is done in a heated room with 45 minutes spent in doing standing poses and 45 minutes for floor poses. The movements help you keep in shape and at the same time, boost your mental concentration to help your physical state become one with your spiritual self.

2. Forrest Yoga

This yoga practice celebrates strength by releasing your emotional and physical tension. It is composed of tough physical movements and emotional exercises. The movements help in clearing your baggage to make enough room to welcome your spirit.

3. Ashtanga Yoga

This yoga, which is athletic in nature, teaches you the value of practicing and setting your mind that good things are coming. Your trainer will design exercises and movements depending on your strengths. You are only required to observe and follow without rejecting.

4. Baptiste Power Vinyasa Yoga

This yoga, which is physically demanding, is also done in a heated room. It requires 90 minutes comprised of vigorous sequences. It aims to help you in coping with the challenges that you may face in the future. The movements were designed to give you the freedom and attain a certain power to accept who you really are while having a peace of mind.

5. Iyengar Yoga

This yoga is perfect for beginners whose movements are still limited. It is comprised of subtle actions with the focus on proper alignment. It gives you a peek of the various movements that you can do in yoga. It also makes you aware of your physical capabilities, strengths, and weaknesses. After learning your body's limitations, this yoga will help in improving your flexibility.

6. Jivamukti Yoga

This is both physically exhilarating and intellectually stimulating. The focus is on the spiritual growth of the practitioner. It includes meditation, breathing techniques, and movements from different yoga practices.

7. Integral Yoga

This yoga helps you go back to your natural state with a clear mind, a heart full of love, and a happy and contented life. The movements are gentle, and it also includes meditation, chanting, and breathing exercises.

8. Sivananda Yoga

This yoga was inspired by the teachings of Swami Sivananda. It is known to be more spiritual than physical. Every session lasts for 90 minutes, wherein you'll be required to do 12 core poses, meditate, relax, and practice pranayama and Sanskrit chanting. It focuses on the five fundamental points of yoga – proper breathing, right exercise, corpse pose, positive thinking and meditation, and vegetarianism or proper diet. The yoga practice aims in helping the practitioner attain a higher level of consciousness.

9. Svaroopa Yoga

Svaroopa, a term that means the bliss of your own being, aims to help you in releasing tension to get rid of those factors that hinder you from having an inner transformation. Each session includes many floor and hand exercises. It starts and ends with the Corpse pose or Savasana.

10. TriYoga

The movements involved in this yoga practice aim to awaken your prana. Each session requires the performance of mudras, flowing asanas, Dharana, pranayama, and meditation. It teaches you spine movements and coordinated breathing.

11. Ishta Yoga

ISHTA or Integrated Science of Hatha, Tantra, and Ayurveda, is a yoga practice that balances the human organism to help you develop a stronger platform to attain spiritual growth. The movements give out varying energetic effects. It aligns your body, teaches you proper breathing techniques, hones your focus through meditation, and cleanses your inner being.

12. Kripalu Yoga

This yoga practice awakens the natural life force to help you in coping with all areas of your life. This can be extremely easy or tough. You'll be required to observe the sensations of your body and mind. This will give you time to understand the nature of the poses and how your body is benefitting from them. It also helps you realize how the decisions you make impact your life. The practice includes meditation, relaxation, asana, and pranayama.

13. Kundalini Yoga

Each session lasts for 90 minutes comprised of extensive movements aimed to push your body and mind to the limits. It typically begins with a chant and ends with the class singing. This yoga style, also referred to as the Yoga of Awareness, includes breathing exercises, mantras, mudras, and mini-meditations – all aimed in awakening your kundalini energy.

As you go about the process, you will experience spiritual evaluation that will lead to the transformation of your core.

14. Prana Flow Yoga

This yoga practice, which is both challenging and empowering, is a fluid form of Vinsaya yoga. It teaches you to connect with prana. Each session typically opens with Om and followed by creative near-continuous sequences with accompanying music.

15. Purna Yoga

Each session starts and ends with quick meditations intended to connect to your heart center. It aims to connect your body and mind to your spirit. The practice is composed of four limbs – pranayama, asana, nutrition, and lifestyle, and applied philosophy. This yoga practice is focused on the asanas combined with yogic philosophy and the alignment methods of Iyengar yoga.

16. OM Yoga

This yoga practice helps the practitioner achieve strength, clarity, and stability. It also helps you develop compassion with how you live your life. The movements, mostly composed of Vinsaya sequences, are done at a moderate pace aligned with compassion and mindfulness.

17. ParaYoga

This yoga practice boosts your self-awareness. It teaches you about how asana affects your energy and how you can develop a more refined prana. Each session is composed of the combination of a dynamic practice and tantric philosophy. You will be required to perform difficult asanas, mudras, bandhas, pranayama, and meditation.

18. Viniyoga

The purpose of this therapeutic yoga is to help you reach the point of discriminative awareness that is important in achieving self-transformation. The sequences were designed to coordinate the movements of the spine with your breathing. It teaches you to focus and cultivate the positive aspects of life and eliminate the negativities.

In deciding which style of yoga to pursue, you have to weigh the benefits of the process and choose the type that is best suited to your health, needs, and physical capabilities. If you don't want to join classes, you can still practice yoga on your own as long as you have the right guide, materials, equipment, and handy tools for first aid.

Benefits of Yoga

Yoga helps you become one with the universe through different techniques, poses, and practices involved.

1. It helps you develop stronger muscles that will reduce the risks of developing back pain and arthritis.

2. It boosts your bone health. As you progress with the practice, you will learn how to lift your own weight. Yoga reduces the levels of the stress hormone in your body and as a result, the calcium in the bones remains intact. The practice reduces your risk of osteoporosis and other bone diseases.

3. Yoga exercises help you in developing a better body posture. Poor posture can lead to health issues in the different areas of the body, including your neck, joint, back, and muscles.

4. The exercises will improve your body's flexibility through continued practice.

5. Aside from achieving enlightenment, yoga also helps you burn calories and stay fit.

6. It helps you stay focused.

7. The exercises boost blood flow and allow more oxygen to get into your system. Yoga reduces your risk of stroke and heart attack.

8. A well-balanced asana practice will result in a more flexible spinal disc since you will do lots of twists, forward and backbends.

9. Yoga helps in keeping your blood pressure normal and maintaining a regular heart rate. It protects you from heart ailments and depression.

10. It decreases the cortisol levels in your system. The opposite will cause health problems, such as insulin resistance, osteoporosis, high blood pressure, and depression.

11. It increases your system's good cholesterol (HDL) and decreases the levels of your bad cholesterol (LDL).

12. Yoga is calming and relaxing. It is a good form of meditation when you are faced with problems and stressors.

13. Your proprioception or your ability to feel where in space is your physical body and what is it doing improves as you do yoga more often. Through time and practice, you will develop a better balance and you will find it easier to perform the difficult yoga sequences.

14. The exercises in yoga require the joints to move in a full range motion. It helps the bones to become strong and less prone to injuries even as you age.

15. The yoga sequences, breathing, and meditation boost the body's immune system.

Chapter 11 - The Mudras and Basic Poses in Yoga

In the ancient Yoga Sutras of Patanjali, physical postures constitute one of eight limbs of yoga. The other limbs include breathing, conduct, and the power of the mind. All these limbs aim to bring out your divine inner qualities.

As you make yoga part of your lifestyle, you will understand how important is the practice to understand your inner self or who you are from within. All human beings have a physical and non-physical existence composed of different layers. Yoga aims to open and activate the principles that will hone each of these layers. To deal with the physical practices of yoga, you have to learn more about the asanas, mudras, and bandhas.

- Asanas – the physical poses, postures, and seats you need to learn to attain spiritual growth and a healthier nervous system.

- Bandhas – physical poses, which are static most of the time. They are geared in improving the areas of the body that block the flow of neurobiological energies from deep within. Yoga will teach you how to direct the energy to flow in the right direction and where it is needed.

- Mudras – composed of physical and dynamic poses geared to the areas of your body that channel the flow of the neurobiological energies to your core.

Among the three, asanas are more known worldwide and are being integrated into various exercises and physical fitness activities. In a way, they help in keeping the interest of many people in yoga.

Mudras and bandhas are separate practices with similarities and overlaps. They are both inward in terms of appearance and performance. They both train the natural physical processes in your core to awaken the Kundalini, where you will experience spiritual ecstasy.

Asanas, mudras, and bandhas are the three major ways in yoga in which you can connect your physical state and spirit.

More about the Mudras

Mudra is a Sanskrit word that means gesture or attitude. In yoga, mudras are performed in combination with breathing exercises to boost the flow of prana and stimulate all parts of the body involved in breathing. These mudras are often taught in the lesser-known and independent branch of yoga known as the Yoga Tatva Mudra Vigyan. The goal is to create a subtle connection with the instincts that affect your unconscious reflexes as you do the movements.

The mudras direct your focus to the gesture being done by your hands as you perform yoga poses. Mudras are also called seals and their goal is to create prana or pathways for energy by unblocking the chakras.

They also have healing effects since the hands have reflexology points and acupressure. Certain mudras are also symbolic in nature.

In yoga, the fingers and toes are believed to be charged with divine power. A mudra is a gesture that looks like a hand pantomime based on the rituals and carries a visual message similar to a hieroglyph. There are many types of mudras ranging from simple to complex.

Here are the most common mudras typically used in Hatha yoga:

1. Gyan Mudra. Relax your fingers. Move your thumb and forefinger closer and press them firmly while keeping the rest of the fingers straight. When doing this mudra in a cross-legged pose, lay the backs of your hands on your thighs. This is also called Jnana mudra or knowledge mudra, which symbolizes connection and oneness.

This mudra affects wisdom. It is done to meditate and disassociate oneself from the material world. It boosts the air element of the body and prompts creative thinking, enthusiasm, and eagerness. When done properly, this mudra can help in boosting your memory and the cognitive process of thinking. It can also relieve depression, drowsiness, and mental retardation.

2. Anjali Mudra. This is the most common mudra, which is also known as the prayer or Namaste position. Press your left palm with your right palm. The pose is said to bring harmony to the right and left sides of your brain. The pose gives instant calmness as long as it is done right.

3. Garuda Mudra. The pose, which resembles a bird, has the same origin as the eagle pose or Garudasana. It has an invigorating effect and it promotes balance. Cross your wrists with your palms to the direction of your chest. Hook the thumbs of your two hands together.

4. Vishnu Mudra. The pose is usually done when performing Nadi Sodhana or alternate nostril breathing. Put your index and middle fingers towards the direction of your palm. With the two fingers bent, keep the rest of the fingers extended.

5. Lotus Mudra. Put your hands together until your palms meet similar to the Anjali mudra. Gradually separate the middle parts of the palms as you spread your fingers without disconnecting your thumbs, pinkies, and the bases of your palms. The pose, reminiscent of the shape of a lotus flower, symbolizes openness and blossoming.

6. Dhyana Mudra. This classic Buddhist meditation pose is done by sitting down as you relax your whole body. Place your left hand on your lap with the palm facing up. Put your right hand on top of the left as you let your thumbs touch the top part of your palms.

7. Kundalini Mudra. This pose, assimilated with one's sexuality and unity, is done by forming a fist in your left hand as you keep the index finger extended. Grip that index finger with your right hand as you form a fist with this hand. Keep the thumb of your right hand lying on top of the index finger of your left hand.

Chapter 12- Mastering Yoga Poses

The first thing you need to do is to familiarize yourself with the proper ways of performing right mudra for each yoga pose suitable for beginners. You can start with the following three poses:

1. Toe Stand (Pandangustasana)

This pose, which is typically performed in Bikram yoga, helps in opening the hips and in strengthening the core of the feet. Perform hip stretches before doing the pose. Be careful with your movements, especially if you have knee problems. If the pain doesn't go away no matter how careful you are, stop doing the pose and perform other poses more suitable for your condition.

Stand in a half lotus tree pose. Stand on your right leg. Move the top of your left foot towards your right hip. Maintain your balance by taking several breaths. Slowly bend your right knee while keeping the left foot on top of the left thigh.

Start lifting your right heel until you are up on the ball of your right foot. Go on a squatting position while keeping your right heel in the center of your body. Make sure that you don't move the right heel under the right buttock.

While in that position, extend your fingertips to the floor ahead of you to attain more balance. Make your belly firm as you lift one hand or both, if you can, off the floor. As you do this, keep your balance on the ball of your right foot. Once you have achieved the perfect balance, move your hands and perform Anjali mudra.

Hold the pose as you inhale and exhale deeply for five counts. Gradually rise back to the half lotus tree pose. Rest for a while as you focus on your breathing. Shake both legs and perform the same sequence to the other side.

If you are having difficulty doing the half lotus pose, you can squat with your heels lifted and your knees together while keeping your balance. This may be difficult in the beginning, but you will eventually get used to it. Once you can do the pose effortlessly, try making it more challenging by coming in and out of the pose without allowing your hands touch the floor.

2. Deep Side Lunge (Skandasana)

You can do this pose in different ways depending on your capability. You can do this with one foot hooked at the back of your head while on a seated forward bend. You can also do the pose with the foot hooked behind your head while standing. The exercise works on your hips and hamstrings and improves your balance and core strength.

Start in a wide-legged forward bend or Prasarita Padottanasana. Gently bend your knee to a half squat. Keep your right leg straight as you extend your foot and lift your toes from the floor. Let your weight rest on your right heel. You can keep your hands on the floor if you are finding it hard to attain balance.

Once you are used with the pose, do it while bending your elbows as you bring your hands together to perform an Anjali mudra pose. Place your left elbow at the inner part of the left knee. Drop your hands to the floor for support as you gradually remove yourself from the pose. Rest for a while and focus on your breathing. Repeat the sequence on the other side.

Most beginners find it hard to get into a full squat. You will eventually get used to it through continued practice. While you still can't, keep standing on the ball of the left foot.

3. Revolved Lunge (Parivrtta Anjaneyasana)

This detoxifying pose requires flexibility, balance, and strength. By twisting your body, you will wring out your internal organs and give your chest enough room to breathe by the end of the pose.

Start in a regular lunge pose. Put your hands down and gradually twist to the right by stepping your left foot backward. You will end up in a high lunge pose with your knee directly facing your ankle and your toes facing forward. Reach through the back heel to make your weight stable and attain balance. Bring your hands to Anjali mudra in front of your chest and twist your body to the right.

Place your elbow and press it outside of the knee. Put your hands together and place them in the middle part of your chest. It is only usual to find it difficult to put your elbow down to your knee in the beginning, but you will eventually get used to it. For beginners, you can retain one hand in prayer position while the other arm is extended.

In case you're finding it difficult to sustain your balance, keep the back of your knee down with your toes tucked underneath. As a beginner, it is more important to keep your lower back safe than to perform fluid movements.

You can perform the twist in a low lunge pose to make it more comfortable or by twisting your rib cage while keeping the belly button up. Keep your chin a little bit tucked as you reach the crown of your head. Come out of the pose by doing the lunge position with your hands down. Step forward and roll up as gently as you can.

A Deeper Look into the Mudras

Aside from simplest forms of mudras already mentioned, there are many more types that range from rare to contemporary and done in various yoga practices.

There are also other mudras that people naturally do without realizing it. The most common example is touching your fingers to your hands, a gesture that brings a subtle change in your attitude and perception. It has a certain power that can affect and heal your body.

The yoga mudras have a direct relationship with the five elements of the human body. This concept is further explained in Ayurveda. According to Ayurveda, a disease is caused by an imbalance in the body that can either be due to the lack or excess of the five elements of the body. These five elements are found in the fingers, which make your fingers important electrical circuits. The role of the mudras is to adjust the flow of energy in the five elements of the body to imbibe healing.

It is important to learn about the five elements of the body because they are used not only in yoga but in a variety of healing techniques, including sound healing and meditation. Here are five elements important in attaining balance and healing:

1. Earth

This element represents the foundation of life and is strongly linked to the root chakra. It deals with emotions of insecurity and failure and basic structures of life, such as money, housing, body contact, work, and partnership. Its basic qualities include solidity, permanence, stability, and heaviness on one's environmental, physical, and mental state.

Too much of this element will make you feel heavy and sleepy. If you are experiencing sleeping problems, here's an exercise that can help you in dealing with it: Lie down in bed while keeping your mind's focus on your feet. Do it for 10 minutes or until you are fully aware of your feet. Use your imagination and think that you are no longer in the room but rather on a beach and your feet are covered by warm and soft sand.

The root chakra is also associated with a human's sense of smell. Newborn babies, for example, know the familiar smell of their mothers' breasts and milk. The baby feels secured upon recognizing the smell of their mother. This familiarity started when the baby was still inside the womb where the first two senses develop, sense of smell and sense of taste.

The way to strengthen the earth element is to imagine or envision. You have to take some time to focus on the image you want to envision and feel the connection.

2. Water

The water element of the body encompasses the sacrum to the point below the navel, an area comprised of a large percentage of water. Getting connected with the water element will boost your creativity, vitality, and sexuality. It will make you feel like you want to get reunited with the mother ocean, an emotion that started whole you were growing in the water inside of your mother's womb.

The basic emotion of the water element is anger. The tendency is to get frustrated and mad when the element is blocked. The energy of fire will help in releasing the negative emotions in the water element. If you are angry, for example, you will feel better after letting your steam off.

3. Fire

This element is found between the navel and beneath the sternum. Its basic emotions are love and understanding. You need to use the other elements to control fire in a productive manner. Use the container the earth element provides to give you fuel and strength. Use the water element to slow it down or extinguish the fire and the air element to stimulate it.

4. Air

The element is found at the bottom to the top of your ribcage, including the heart, lungs, and the thymus gland. A person gets depressed when the energy of the heart chakra is held close to the chest and cannot expand. Depression, the opposite of joy, is a sign of longing for something higher. To feel lighter and inspired, you have to do something for the heart chakra to expand freely. This element knows your passion and what makes you happy.

5. Space

This element, also called the ether, does not have a shape or color and fills the gap between objects and people. Nothing will exist without space and its absence will make you appreciate its importance. Its main characteristic is silence.

This element offers ultimate security because unlike Earth, it won't disintegrate nor carried away by wind or water. This is found from the collar bones to the bridge of the nose, the area of the body called the point of silence. It encompasses the mouth, eyes, ears, nose, and vocal cords.

The characteristics of these five elements are found in your fingers. Performing the mudras will adjust the flow of energy in your body to balance the five elements and promote healing.

There are basically two kinds of mudras in yoga. The first one involves the touching of the tips of different fingers with the thumb. The second one is pressing the first phalangeal joint with the thumb. The effects of the mudras depend on which fingers are touching or being pressed.

Additional Mudras to Know About

Here are the other mudras that you can do after you are done with the basic ones. You can do the following while doing yoga poses, such as cross-legged or lotus, or while seated on a chair:

1. Adi Mudra

Place your thumb at the base of your small finger while keeping the rest of the fingers curled over the thumb forming a light fist. Place your hands on your thighs with the palms facing up. Breathe deeply and be attentive how the mudra affects you.

2. Brahma Mudra

Position your hands similar to Adi Mudra. Place the knuckles of your hands together and place them in the navel area. Breathe deeply up to 12 counts. Be mindful of the flow of your breathing and how it affects your mind and body.

3. Chin mudra

Lightly touch each of your thumbs with your forefingers. Keep the rest of the fingers extended and straight. You can place your hands on top of your thighs with the palms facing up. Breathe deeply and focus on its flow. Relax and don't exert pressure on your fingers and hands.

4. Chinmaya Mudra

Form a ring with your thumb and forefinger and curl the three remaining fingers in your palm. Place your hands on your thighs with palms facing up. Take deep ujjayi breaths as you relax your whole body. Focus on your breathing and its effects.

5. Vaayu Mudra

This mudra is also called Vaayu Shaamak Mudra – Vaayu meaning air and Shaamak means to suppress. It helps in soothing your emotions. Put the tip of your index finger at the base of your thumb. Press the two fingers lightly as you breathe deeply.

This mudra decreases the air element in your body. It soothes your spirit and calms your mind. It also pacifies the nervous system and heals hormonal imbalance. This is recommended for people who are hyperactive, aggressive and have difficulty in keeping their focus.

6. Aakash Mudra

This mudra, meaning or space and Vardhak or to enhance, gives you a feeling of lightness. Gently touch the tips of your middle finger with the thumb to boost the space element in your body. For best results, perform this mudra from 2 to 6 in the morning or afternoon. Do not do this for more than 30 minutes each session if you have an active body.

It eases away your negative thoughts and worries and helps in dealing with anger, sadness, and fear. It has a detoxifying effect and is ideal for those who have problems with congestion, tummy, ear, sinus, and chest.

7. Shunya Mudra

This mudra also called Aakash Shaamak Mudra – Aakash meaning space and Shaamak meaning to suppress, has a healing effect for pains. It also decreases the space element in your body. Gently touch the tip of your middle finger at the base of your thumb and give it a slight press.

It prevents the feeling of numbness in your chest and head. It also helps in relieving ear-related pains, such as minor aches, tinnitus, impaired hearing, travel sickness, and nausea. You can perform this mudra any time you want. If you are doing this to get rid of earaches, numbness, and vertigo, make sure that you stop when the pain has subsided.

8. Prithvi Mudra

This mudra is also called Prithvi Vardhak Mudra – Prithvi means earth and Vardhak means to enhance, and Agni Shaamak Mudra – Agni means fire and Shaamak means to suppress. This is said to affect a person's strength and vitality.

Touch the tips of your ring finger to your thumb. This simple action decreases the fire element in your body while boosting the earth element. It allows you to heal, build muscles and encourage the growth of new tissue. It helps in boosting your energy and is effective for those who are suffering from dry skin and brittle nails, hair, and bones. It can also regulate the body temperature and metabolic process. This is recommended to skinny people and those who often experience ulcers, fever, and inflammation.

9. Surya Mudra

This mudra is also called Prithvi Shaamak Mudra – Prithvi means earth and Shaamak means to suppress and Agni Vardhak Mudra – Agni means fire and Vardhak means to enhance. It works by decreasing the earth element while increasing the fire element in your system. This is recommended when you are shivering due to low temperature and colds. Place the tip of your ring finger at the base of your thumb and gently press.

This is a good mudra for those who want to lose weight. It aids in digestion and deals with health concerns, such as constipation, lack of appetite, and suppressed thyroid activity. This can be done at any time during the day for 30 minutes or less for each session. Doing this mudra longer than 30 minutes will cause your body to overheat.

10. Varun Mudra

This is also called Jal Vardhak Mudra – Jal means war and Vardhak means to enhance. Gently touch the tips of your little finger with your thumb. The simple movement has a moisturizing effect and is recommended for those who are suffering from general dehydration, cramps, and hormonal deficiency.

It works by increasing the water element in your body. It also helps in relieving joint pains, arthritis, and improves the condition of those who have lost the sensation of taste and experience limited body secretions. It also deals with dry hair, eyes and skin, digestive health problems, and eczema. This is safe for everybody except for people who have problems with water retention.

11. Jal Shaamak Mudra

This mudra, which is intended for stability, means Jal for water and Shaamak or to suppress. Place the tip of your little finger to the base of the thumb and gently press.

It works by decreasing the water element in the body. This is recommended for people who have problems with water retention or edema, hyperacidity, too much glandular secretion, watery eyes, sweaty palms, runny nose, and too much salivation.

Chapter 13 – How to Relax and Meditate Through Yoga

A big part of learning in Buddhism is meditation and exercises aimed to give you calmness and enlightenment. After knowing about the mudras and the basic yoga poses, you can expand your knowledge and test your strength by doing the more complicated poses.

Asanas, which is one of the eight limbs of yoga, are now being practiced worldwide and have been adapted in the physical fitness industry. Asanas or physical postures are important in executing other styles of yoga. They are defined by types, benefits, anatomy, and many more.

There are many kinds of asanas and they depend on your initial pose upon doing the exercise and your purpose for the poses. These poses include standing, arm balance, balancing poses, binding, chest opening, core yoga poses, forward bend, hip opening, inversion, pranayama, restorative, seated, strengthening, twist, backbends, and bandha.

Before giving an example of a good yoga sequence for relaxation and meditation, you must first learn how to perform the warm-up exercises. Warming up is an essential part not only of yoga but all other kinds of exercises.

The warm-up yoga exercises depend upon the parts of the body you'll use during the exercise. Always make sure that the movements are gentle, and fluid and you always focus on your deep breathing.

Warm-up exercises for the whole body:

1. Start in Easy Pose or Sukhasana. Sit on the floor with your legs crossed. Make sure that your buttocks are comfortable. Put your feet below your knees. Place your hands on your lap with the palms facing downwards or upwards. Move your hip bones to the mat as you reach your hands on top of your head. Slowly drop your shoulders as you push your chest in front. Relax your face and stomach as you breathe through the nose. Hold the pose as long as you can.

2. Breathe in as you extend your fingertips in the direction of the ceiling.

3. Breathe out and let your palms rest on the mat.

4. Repeat steps 2 and 3. Twist your body to the left upon breathing out. Repeat and twist your body to the right. Repeat and upon breathing out, arch your body to the left. Repeat and arch your body to the right. Inhale and put your arms behind you. Breathe out as you lay your hands on the mat.

5. Bring your spine to a neutral pose with the shoulders down, the spine extended and your chest open.

Repeat the warm-up before you begin doing other yoga poses.

For the neck:

1. Begin the sequence by doing any seated pose. Keep your shoulders laid back, your spine extended and chest open. Breathe out as you lay your chin to your chest. Breathe in as you put your neck back to the center.

2. Breathe out and lay your head backward. Keep your shoulders down as you lift your chin and relax your mouth. Breathe in as you put your neck back to the center.

3. Breathe out as you move the lower part of your left ear to your left shoulder. Breathe in as you put your neck back to the center. Repeat the step on the other side.

4. Breathe out as you extend your chin to your left shoulder. With your body faced in front, gently twist your neck and look at any point behind you. Breathe in as you put your neck back to the center. Repeat the step on the other side.

For the shoulders:

1. Start by doing the Easy Pose.

2. Breathe in as you extend your arms in the direction of the ceiling. Intertwine your fingers and move your palms upward. Breathe out and arch your body to the left.

3. Breathe in as you extend your palms to the ceiling while keeping your hips grounded to the mat. Breathe out and arch your body to the right.

4. Breathe in as you reach your palms upward. Breathe out as you round your spine by pressing your hands to the front.

5. Breathe in as you extend your palms upward. Breathe out as you bend your right elbow on the back of your head. Repeat the step on your left elbow.

6. Breathe in as you extend your palms to the ceiling. Breath out as you slowly put your hands down.

7. Breathe in and make slow and large circles as you roll your shoulders up and down to the front and then to the back. Breathe out as you lay your knees to the mat.

A Sample Yoga Sequence to Help You Relax

Here is an example of a yoga sequence you can perform every day. This is aimed to calm your mind and train your brain to relax and was based on the teachings of the Mindful Yoga Therapy. The sequence is commonly used to help returning military service members suffering from the post-traumatic stress disorder.

The focus of the exercise is on the present and you will do this through proper movements and breathing. Your mind should focus on the moment and avoid thinking about the past or future. Through continued practice, you will notice the change in your attitude and the way you think.

To accomplish the goal and help you relax, perform the following poses:

1. Constructive Rest

Lie with your back on the mat while keeping your knees bent and your feet apart. Put your knees together to allow them to rest. Close your eyes and breathe. Focus on your breathing as you allow the breath to move through your body. Use your imagination to guide the breath as it travels to the body to nourish your organs, cells, and tissues.

If you are feeling any kind of pain, draw your mind to the spot. Breathe in and imagine the fresh oxygen washing away the pain. Exhale all the causes of the pain away from you.

Imagine a thing or person you are fond of. Focus on the image as your reason for doing the sequence. Do this part for as long as you like. You can also cut it short if you are certain that you have already achieved your set goal.

2. Supine Twist

This pose helps ease the tension on your lower back. Place your knees closer to your chest as you rest your right hand on your left knee. Extend your left arm straight out to the left. Breathe in and focus on your breathing. Breathe out and carefully roll your knees to the right. Take five breaths. Breathe in and put your knees back to the middle. Breathe out and squeeze your knees back to your chest. Breathe in and extend your left hand on your right knee. Stretch out your right arm. Breathe out and move your knees to the left. Take five breaths.

Breathe in and move your knees to the middle and squeeze them for the last time. Breathe out and release your feet to the floor. Twist deeper by reaching to your extended arm. This will push more air to your lungs.

3. Hands and Knees Balance

Listen to your body as you let it rest. When it is ready for this step, roll your body to one side and sit. Go down to the floor on your hands and knees. Place your hands a little bit in front of your shoulders and your knees under your hips. Focus your attention to your hands. Press your hands down to the earth. This pose intends to keep you grounded and remain at the moment.

Gently bend your elbows. Keep pressing to continue connecting with the earth. Get support from the floor or earth to remain grounded. Develop an instinct that you will get support whenever you need it.

Imagine there is an extra hand holding your navel and giving support on the underside of your body. Lift your core slowly and move it inward. The movement intends to support, protect, and strengthen the lower portions of your back. Be mindful in keeping this support throughout the exercise.

Breathe in and extend the right arm and left leg into the hands and knees pose. Grasp both of your limbs in contrasting routes to keep your body steady and even. Hold the pose as you take five breaths. Breathe out and move your extended arm and leg to the floor. Repeat the movements on the other side.

4. Plank Pose

Move your feet until you are in a Plank Pose with your hands directly under your shoulders. Straighten your body until it is similar to a long and even line. Press your hands through the earth and feel its rebound through your tailbone. Allow your senses to feel the connection from your head to your heels while you gather strength from the navel. Keep your collarbones and chest wide and do not allow your hips to hang. Take five easy Ujjayi breaths.

5. Downward-Facing Dog Pose (Adho Mukha Svanasana)

Knees and hands on the floor with your hands aligned under your shoulders. Push the earth with force using your hands. Curl your toes under and gently bend your knees. Push your body back until you are in an Adho Mukha Svanasana pose.

Focus on your hands firmly pressed to the ground and then to your sitting bones. Keep the navel support for strength as you stretch both sides of your waist. If you have tight hamstrings, bend your knees. Take up to 10 breaths. Move your hands to your feet. Breathe in and stand up.

6. Warrior Pose II (Virabhadrasana II)

Step your feet sideways until they are about 4 feet apart. Establish your footwork to give you support while making sure that you maintain the navel support. Twist your right leg and foot to the right. Move your back leg and foot slightly backward. Your right heel has to be in line with the arch of your left foot. Focus your attention on the ground through your legs and feet.

Breathe in as you extend your arms to your sides. Breathe out as you bend your right knee. Move your right sitting bone in the direction of your right foot. Do not allow your knee to go beyond your ankle. You will find stability through your back leg. Focus on your back leg and take 5 breaths. Keep yourself grounded. Breathe in and push to the floor. Extend your right leg and release the posture. Breathe out as you go back to the middle. Repeat the movements on your left side.

7. Extended Triangle Pose (Utthita Trikonasana)

Twist your right leg and foot out. Take your time as you align your feet similar to the previous pose. Breathe in, push your feet to the floor and extend your arms to your sides. From your feet, shift your focus through the crown of your head. Breathe out and use the navel support to keep your spine extended and healthy. Stretch out the right side of your body over your right leg. Reach your shin with your right hand.

Allow your left arm to extend to the sky. Take 5 breaths. Maintain the Ujjayi breath. As you breathe out, go back to the middle. Repeat the actions on your left side.

8. Tree Pose (Vrksasana)

Keep your gaze (Drishti) on one point to keep your body steady. Push your feet to the floor as you draw awareness from your heels to the crown of your head while maintaining navel support. Lift your right foot and press it against the left leg. Keep your foot above or below the knee. Push your leg back into your foot to create a contrasting feeling.

Put your palms together and bring it in front of your heart. Extend your arms to the sky while imagining that they were growing limbs of a tree. Find peace and make yourself calm. Keep your focus on your breathing and Drishti even when you feel like the tree is swaying. Take up to 10 breaths and repeat on the other side.

9. Supported Shoulder-stand (Salamba Sarvangasana)

Lie with your back on the floor and keep your feet and knees hip-distance apart. Breathe in and push your feet down as you begin lifting your hips. Turn on your shoulder tops and use a block to support your sacrum or the triangular bone found at the base of your spine. Place the block under the sacrum at the point where you are comfortable with its height.

Put your hands to your sides and push them to the floor. Move your chin in the direction of your chest. Refrain from moving your head from side to side. As you breathe out, pull your right knee to your chest. Breathe in and stretch your right leg. Take 5 breaths. Breathe out and pull your right knee back in. Breathe in and move your right foot back to the floor. Breathe out and pull your left knee to your chest. Breathe in and stretch your left leg upward. Take 5 breaths.

Breathe out and pull your left knee back in. Leave it there as you pull your right knee to meet with the other knee. When your feet are on the floor, focus on the support from your hands and the block under your sacrum. Breathe in as you extend your legs upward. Hold the pose for 5 breaths.

Pull both knees to your chest and allow them to come down as you breathe out. Breathe in and put your feet on the ground and pressed firmly on the floor. Lift your hips and remove the block. Gently allow your body to go back to the earth and take your moment until your spine has adjusted.

10. Corpse Pose (Savasana)

Lie with your back on the floor. Extend your legs and arms with your palms facing up. As an option, you can place a bolster under your knees if it gives you comfort. You can also perform the exercise without the prop by finding a posture you are comfortable with. Soften your gaze or close your eyes. Hold for at least 5 minutes. Draw your focus to your every movement.

The Asanas or Yoga Poses

Yoga asanas are important in executing other yoga styles. The kinds of asanas depend on your initial pose when doing the exercise and what you aim to achieve.

Samples of Standing Yoga Poses

1. Big Toe Pose (Padangusthasana)

Stand straight with the inner part of your feet parallel and about 6 inches apart from each other. Contract the front muscles of your thigh as you move your kneecaps upwards. Make sure that your legs remain straight as you breathe out. Do a forward bend from the hip joints to your torso and head.

Slide the index and middle fingers of your two hands in between the big toes and the second toes. Curl your fingers under, firmly gripping your big toes. Wrap the thumbs around the other two fingers to make the grip more secure and press the toes against the fingers.

Breathe in, lift your torso and extend your elbows as if you are going to stand up. Stretch the front part of your torso, exhale and lift your sitting bones. Carefully release your hamstrings and the hollow the part below your navel and lift it slightly towards the back part of your pelvis.

Keep your forehead relaxed as you lift your sternum as high as you can. Make sure that you don't overdo the action to avoid compressing the back of your neck.

Inhale as lift your torso strongly while contracting your front thighs. On the next exhalations, forcefully lift your sitting bones, let your hamstrings relax and make the hollow in your lower back deeper.

Exhale and bend your elbows to the sides. Pull up on your toes and stretch the front and sides of your torso. Lower the torso in a gentle manner by doing a forward bend.

Hold the position for one minute. Lose the grip on your toes. Place your hands to your hips and stretch your front torso. Inhale and swing your torso and head as if you are dealing with a single unit and go back to an upright pose.

2. Mountain Pose (Tadasana)

Stand straight with the bases of your big toes touching and the second toes in line with each other. Lift and spread your toes. Move the balls of your feet before putting them back again to the floor. Move your feet to the front and back and then from side to side to rock your weight. Gradually reduce the frequency of the swaying of your body until you are standing still. Carry your weight on your feet to give you balance.

Lift your kneecaps with your thigh muscles remaining firm and your lower belly relaxed. Lift the inner parts of your ankles. Imagine your inner thighs with a line of energy that runs through the groin to the torso, neck, up to the crown of your head. Move the upper parts of your thighs inward. Extend your tailbone to the floor and lift your pubis to the direction of the navel.

Keep the shoulder blades at the back before gradually spreading them across and releasing them to your back. Lift the top part of the sternum in the direction of the ceiling without pushing your ribs forward. Spread your collarbones and let your arms hang at each side of your torso.

Make sure that the top of your head is balanced. Keep your chin resting on the floor. Keep the pose for a minute as you breathe easily.

3. Dolphin Pose (Ardha Pincha Mayurasana)

This position opens your shoulders by working on your core, arms, and legs. Come down on the floor on your hands and knees, forearms on the floor and shoulders above your wrists. Press your palms together in a firm manner.

Curl your toes. Exhale and slowly raise your knees in a slightly bent manner and the heels away. Extend your tailbone and slightly press it in the direction of your pubis. Lift the sitting bones upward and draw your inner legs up to your groins.

Keep your forearms pressed to the floor while your shoulder blades are firm against the back. Extend the blades and draw them in the direction of your tailbone. Continue to extend your tailbone away from the pelvis as you lift the upper part of the sternum away from the floor. Hold position for up to a minute. Release your knees as you exhale.

4. Chair Pose (Utkatasana)

This position utilizes the muscles in your legs and arms and provides health benefits to your heart and diaphragm.

Begin by standing in Tadasana. Breathe in as you move your arms upwards until they are perpendicular to the floor. Keep your arms parallel with the palms facing inward. Slowly bend your knees as you exhale. Try to position your thighs parallel to the floor to push your torso slightly forward until it forms a right angle with the top parts of the thighs. Make sure that the inner thighs remain parallel to one another as you press the heads of the bones of your thighs in the direction of your heels.

Relax your shoulder blades until they are firm against your back. Move your tailbone to your pubis while keeping the lower part of the back long. Hold the position for up to a minute. Inhale and straighten your knees as you lift through your arms. Release your arms and put them on each of your sides as you exhale. Go back to Tadasana.

5. Eagle Pose (Garudasana)

This pose works by boosting your endurance, concentration, flexibility, and strength. Begin in the Tadasana pose. Slightly curve your knees and move your left foot in the direction of the ceiling. Keep the right foot balanced as the left thigh crosses over the other thigh. Position the left toes parallel to the floor. Press your foot and hook its upper part at the back of the lower right calf. Maintain your balance using your right foot.

Extend your arms spreading the scapulas across the back part of the torso. Put the right arm at the top of the left arm. Move the right arm in front of your torso and slowly bend your elbows. Put the right elbow into the corner of the left elbow and extend the forearms until they are positioned vertically to the mat. Make sure that the back parts of your hands are facing one another.

Move the palms until they are facing each other. Move the thumb of the right hand beyond the little finger of your left hand. Press your palms together with force. Lift your elbows and spread your fingers upwards. Keep the position for up to 30 seconds. Unwind your arms and legs and go back to the Tadasana pose. Repeat the sequence using the other side of your legs and arms.

Arm Balance Yoga Poses

The following yoga poses are intended to make you stronger, with an improved balance, by challenging yourself and conquering your fear of doing more difficult movements.

1. Eight-Angle Pose (Astavakrasana)

Begin by standing in a Tadasana pose with your feet spread wider than usual. Exhale and change into the Uttanasana pose. Push your hands to the floor outside of your feet. Slightly bend your knees and slide your right arm inside your right leg. Push your hand to the floor outside of your right foot. Place your right arm across the back of your right knee and bring the knee as high as the back of your right shoulder.

Keep your shoulders against the knees as you slide your left foot to the right foot. Cross your left ankle in front of the right and hook them up. Move slightly towards the left as you put more weight on your left arm. Lift your feet several inches away off the floor.

Exhale as you support the right leg with your shoulder and slowly bend your elbows. Lean forward, your torso should be parallel to the floor. Keep the pose as you extend your knees to stretch your legs out to the right while keeping them parallel to the floor. Keep the upper right arm in between your thighs squeezed and tight. Use the pressure to twist your torso to the left. Keep the elbows in proximity with your torso and your gaze to the floor. Hold the pose for up to a minute.

Slowly extend your arms while moving your torso upright. Bend your knees and unhook your ankles. Put your feet back to the floor. As you stand, rest in Uttanasana. Breathe in and breathe out for a few counts. Repeat the sequence to the left.

2. Crane/Crow Pose (Bakasana)

The pose can help in making your arms and abs stronger. Begin in Tadasana. Bend your knees while keeping your feet a few inches away from each other. You can use a prop if you are finding it hard to maintain the balance of your heels. You can place a thick blanket for support. Widen the gap between your two knees as you lean your torso forward. Extend your arms in front. Slowly bend your elbows as you lay your hands on the mat while the back parts of your upper arms are positioned against your shins.

Nestle the inner parts of your thighs against the outer areas of your torso and keep your shins in the armpits. Slide the upper part of your arms until they are close to your shins. Use the balls of your feet as you lift your weight and lean forward to transfer the weight to back parts of your upper arms. Keep your tailbone close to your heels as you perform the movements.

As you exhale, lean forward until the legs and your torso are balanced with the back parts of the upper arms. You can hold this pose if you are a beginner. The more experienced practitioners can continue with the rest of the steps.

Cuddle your legs against your arms and strongly push the inner parts of your hands to the mat. Inhale and stretch your elbows. With your arms slightly angled forward, keep the inner parts of the knees stuck to your arms up to the areas near the sides of your chest. Keep your head comfortable and balanced and your gaze on the floor. Keep the pose for up to a minute. Exhale as you release the pose. Lower your feet to the mat and go back to your original squat position.

3. Four-Limbed Staff Pose (Chaturanga Dandasana)

This position is part of the traditional Sun Salutation sequence. Begin in the Adho Mukha Svanasana and change into the Plank Pose. Keep the shoulder blades firm against your back ribs and push the tailbone to your pubis. As you exhale, lower your torso and legs until they are inches above the floor. Keep your tailbone firm and your legs active and turned in a slight inward manner. Pull your pubis to your navel.

Hold your elbows by the sides of your torso while keeping a broad space between your shoulder blades. Push your elbows back toward your heels. Push the bottom of your index fingers to the floor. Move the top of your sternum and head up as you keep your gaze upfront. Count up to 30 before you exhale as you release and go back up to the Adho Mukha Svanasana pose.

4. Firefly Pose (Tittibhasana)

Stand with your feet a little far apart and then go on a squat. Lift the pelvis a little to the front bringing the trunk in between your legs. Lower the trunk as you extend your legs until your pelvis is of knee height.

Move your left upper arm and shoulder under the back of your left thigh and reach as far as you can. Put your left hand to the floor at the outside corners of your foot while keeping your fingers pointing forward. Repeat the sequence on the other side.

Carefully lift your weight away from the floor. Push your hands to the floor and rock your weight from your feet to your hands keeping your inner thighs as high as you can on your arms.

Inhale as you extend your legs to the sides while keeping the pelvis high. Push through the bottom of your big toes while pulling your toes to your torso and spreading your toes apart.

Stretch your arms and widen your shoulder blades to lift the torso higher. Keep your neck relaxed with your head and gaze looking ahead. Breathe in a slow manner for about 15 minutes as you hold the pose. Release by putting your feet to the floor upon exhale.

5. Peacock Pose (Mayurasana)

This pose symbolizes immortality and love. Kneel on a mat with your knees wide. Lean your body as you push your palms to the floor and your fingers directed to your torso. Slightly bend your elbows as they touch your hands. Bend your elbows as you move your knees away from your arms. Move the front torso on the back of the upper arms. Cradle your elbows at your tummy.

Press your tummy against your elbows as you lower your head to the floor. Extend your knees and straighten your legs at the back of your torso. Keep the tips of your toes on the floor, your buttocks firm and your shoulders round and slightly downward. Slowly lift your head and keep your gaze forward. Transfer your weight a little to the front and lift your feet. Your torso and legs have to be aligned to the floor. Hold the pose for 10 seconds or longer if you can.

Lower down your head and feet to the floor as you bend your knees and lift your torso away from the arms.

Chapter 14 – Center Yourself With Sound Healing

To benefit from sound healing, it is important to learn how to center yourself. Trust the process, develop compassion and keep yourself grounded. These practices are similar to yoga, meditation, and other healing and meditative processes taught in Buddhism.

Sound healing involves all the levels of a person's energy. There are no rules but to follow your instinct on how to deal with your energy fields. The concept came from the notion that a human being is a center of energy subjected to the influences of other energies – color, light, and sound.

Sound is the most powerful energy among the three. Sound therapy focuses on soothing and healing sounds. It gives you a choice which sounds you want to reach your ear and brain. The therapy teaches you how to stay unaffected by noise and other unwanted sounds.

Noise is damaging to the ears and is the main cause of hearing loss. The ear is the first to react to its surroundings. It is also said to be the most sensitive organ both in humans and animals.

Noise gives off an unpleasant sensation and poses harm to the ear structure. A mouse exposed to the sound of a siren for a few seconds will likely suffer from a convulsive audiogenic attack. This serves as proof that noise can be fatal. Noise can cause disequilibrium that harms the nerve centers at the base of the brain.

Sound healing is a conscious and educated use of the energy gathered from sounds. Based on the concept that everything that surrounds you vibrates at specific frequencies; it helps in boosting one's health and wellness to reach identified goals. When an external source of sound plays, it will cause a significant change in the vibrational characteristics of the other objects that vibrate.

Sound healing, aside from being a good meditative technique, also offers the following health benefits:

- Raise one's consciousness
- Personal transformation
- Reduce stress
- Improve sleep disorders
- Enhance the immune system
- Help the patients relax
- Alleviates pain

- Enhance clarity and alertness
- Connect with one's spirit

Learning How to Center Yourself

Here's a brief guide to get this done. This will help you adapt the techniques and other factors important to sound healing.

1. Look for a square area or anything similar. Position yourself in any way you're comfortable with. Breathe deeply as you focus your mind to your navel, spleen, and solar plexus.

2. Feel your surroundings. Keep on breathing deeply as you turn your attention to the area above your head.

3. Turn your attention and look at your legs and feet. Move your toes and feel each movement. Be attentive of each foot until you feel something concrete and you've reached the point when you feel like you are well-grounded.

4. Turn your attention to your heart chakra. Keep on focusing until you are fully aware of it. Allow the feeling of softness spread in the vast space ahead of you.

You can easily apply the other techniques used in the process once you have mastered the art of centering yourself. For sound healing to work, you have to let go of your emotions and ego and allow your intuition and emotion to take charge.

Sound healing works by using silence and different sources of sound, including humming, your own voice, and musical instruments. You will use musical instruments according to their characteristics and the elements they attract. The first thing to do is to set your goal. Ask yourself what you want to achieve in the process. It is typically used for relaxation, to understand the seemingly vague areas of life, learning more about yourself, overcoming pains, and many more.

You also have to be patient whether you are the one undergoing the process, or you are the healer. Healing takes time. Do not expect a miracle to happen in a few hours. Its effects can be felt in different ways and different places and levels.

Another powerful and effective element in sound healing is the use of voice. With a wide range of sounds and letters found in human languages, you will find some sounds linked to the five elements.

Sound healing improves your health and life in general. It allows you to witness your own transformation as you experience the effects of the process. With the right goal and proper implementation of the process, you will experience positive changes and benefits, which include the following:

- Become more focused
- Understand that you are part of a big universe

- Develop a positive outlook in life
- Develop a healthy lifestyle
- Become happier

Sound therapy teaches you to choose what you hear and how to imbibe their effects. Instead of stopping the noise, you can diffuse it by playing a gentle sound. There are many therapies and techniques used in sound healing depending on the training and beliefs of the practitioner and the purpose of healing.

Sound healing is among the oldest forms of healing known to humans. It uses sound frequencies to bring the body and mind in a state of health and harmony. It gets transmitted in different ways, such as:

- Listening to music through earphones or headphones or a loudspeaker
- Listening to one or more instruments
- Use of voice with other voices
- Use of own voice
- Another individual's voice
- Use of own voice while listening to music

The Concepts of Sound Healing

1. Every person has a unique soul or root frequency. You have to get in touch with that frequency to feel the moment, to be grounded, and centered. What makes it hard to connect with the frequency is the distraction caused by the noises in the surroundings. Aside from your core frequency, everything inside you – tissue, vertebrae, organ, muscle, Etheric field, and chakra, has a resonating frequency.

Sound healing helps you become more aware of the symphony inside of you. Through the use of methods, such as toning and vibroacoustic massage – a form of massage in tables with speakers, you will find it easier to maintain a healthy flow of music from deep within.

2. Healing comes from the force behind all things found in the universe and not something that you do. Jonathan Goldman created a formula in 1992 that equates healing as a sum of frequency and intention.

Shamans believed that intent is an indescribable and immeasurable force connected to everything that exists. They refer to it as a universal mind, consciousness, soul, spirit, or source. Its practitioners believe that miracles happen when people become in harmony with the spirit. People align themselves to this universal power through intention.

Everyone has an intention in every action whether you were conscious about it or not. In sound healing, the sound carries this intention to bring back the harmony to your mind, body, spirit, and emotions.

3. Every sound has a harmonic structure. One note from a playing instrument is composed of several notes playing in harmony. The harmonics that constitute a sound are mathematical multiples of the root frequency. They prove that everything is connected and there is a unified field every person is always connected to. Through sound healing, it gets easier to become more aware of this connection.

Sound Healing Principles

Sound healing helps you to connect to a supreme being and your core by following these principles:

1. Entrainment

This principle, discovered by a Dutch scientist, Christian Huygens in 1665, states that when two or more oscillators in the same area are pulsing at about the same rate, they are pulled together and locked in while pulsing at the same rate.

For example, birds fly together during migration. They glide and flap their wings at the same time. They conserve energy by flapping their wings according to the group's rhythm. The bird in front creates a pocket air of turbulence that the other birds use to their advantage to boost the resistance of their flapping wings.

In the human body, the notion is applied when one part of the body is out of tune. Sound healing works by bringing back the balance without the need to take medicines or undergo a surgery or operation.

2. Resonance

This healing technique believes that every organism has its own vibratory rate. Different objects in this universe have a unique resonant frequency that sets them apart from one another. Every cell, bone, and organ in the body has its resonant frequency. Together, they act as the instruments in an orchestra to form a composite frequency. The body experiences something different when one instrument did not work.

Modern medicine utilizes Lithotripter, a machine that employs sound waves to break up the gallstones and kidney in the human body. It sends a specific sound frequency to the stones for an hour or two. In most cases, this will only require one session and can be done without any anesthesia. The stones are efficiently broken and pulverized before getting mixed with urine for the body to get rid of them. The goal of science is to eventually use the resonance principle to get the bodily organs in harmony to avoid surgery and drugs.

3. The healing power of voice

Toning requires the creation of sound with an elongated vowel for a long duration. It helps your breathing to become deeper and for the body to get oxygenated and stimulated.

The elongated vowel sounds, Aaah, Eeee, Eye, Oooo, and Uuuu, are non-specific and non-local. You can recite them while directing the vibration to the body part you wish to address.

You will feel a connection when you tone along with other people. It also offers other benefits, which include the following:

- Energizes your body
- Makes you feel calm and relaxed
- Releases your repressed emotions and stress
- Improves your posture and breathing
- Makes the vocal muscles stronger
- Stimulates the muscles of your digestive system

Toning also has a neurochemical effect on the body. It aids in releasing the endorphins in the brain by boosting your immune system. This is also an effective tool in addressing various sleep disorders, such as insomnia. In the medical field, it helps in reducing the patient's tension before undergoing CAT scans and MRI. It also helps in releasing psychological stress before undergoing surgery and in decreasing the respiratory rate and blood pressure of cardiac patients.

4. Chant

The practice, commonly called kirtan in India, is done by saying words, syllables or phrases over and over again. Chanting is done until the practitioner relaxes, which makes it easier to find inner peace.

It can be as simple as repeating the sounds in any way you are comfortable with. You can begin by chanting the OM sound. Focus on what you want to achieve or what negative energies you want to get rid of. Inhale and as you release your breath, chant the OM sound repeatedly in a loud manner. Inhale and continue chanting as you breathe out. As you go through the process, you will gradually decrease the volume of your voice until it sounds almost like a whisper.

Continue the process until you are repeating the chant silently wherein you no longer move your tongue and lips. Focus on the sound until it leads you into the realm of infinite possibilities. Repeat chanting OM silently at times when your mind wanders. Keep the pose for 15 minutes.

Here are some samples of the chants you can use to focus on your Chakras:

- LAAM – First Chakra, located at the base of the spine
- VAAM – Second Chakra, located in the sacral region
- RAAM – Third Chakra, located at the navel area
- YAAM – Fourth Chakra, located at the heart
- HAAM – Fifth Chakra, located in the throat area
- KSHAAM – Sixth Chakra, in between the eyebrows
- OM – Seventh Chakra, located at the top of the head

Here's a list of the toning sounds you can use to address specific areas of your body or to achieve a specific purpose:

- UU-AH-EE-MM – Gives a boost of energy and helps in keeping you awake
- MM-EE-AH-UU – Relaxes your body, especially during bedtime
- Nnn – For the ears
- Wooo – For the bladder and kidneys
- Mmm – For the sinuses
- Shhh – For the small intestine and liver
- Eemm – For the eyes
- Sssss – For the large intestine and lungs
- Lmm – For the nose
- Ma – For the heart
- Paam – For the stomach
- Mam – For the reproductive organs
- Haa – For the diaphragm
- Yaa Yu Yi – For the jaw
- Kaa Gaa Gha – For the throat

5. Rhythm

A human heartbeat follows the rhythm of the music. Your breathing rate decreases when you hear a slower tempo playing. For example, Pachelbel's Canon has a similar rhythm to the resting heartbeat rate, which is 64 beats per minute. Upon hearing the music, your brain wave pattern changes from Beta to Alpha. In music therapy, patients listen to slow classical music to improve their metabolism and make the nervous system calmer.

6. Drumming

The brain rhythm slows down when it hears repetitive drumming that leads you into a trance-like state. Healing happens when the practitioner and the client get out from the conscious awareness and venture into the realms of consciousness, a technique popularly used in Shamanic practices.

A reticular activating system or RAS is found in the brainstem that makes it possible to get affected when you hear repetitive drumming. The RAS alerts the brain about the incoming sensory stimulation. The sound overpowers the other sensory channels in the brain. It leads to your consciousness exploring other kinds of perception as it suppresses the normal activity of the brain.

Sound Healing and Aura

The first energy field you will sense upon seeing a person is their spiritual aura. This aura is something that everybody has with the qualities that have been likely developed in their past lives. You were born with an aura, but you have to learn how to activate that aura and use it in this lifetime.

In sound healing, you have to focus on your spiritual qualities and set aside your current psychological state. You don't deal with emotional problems head-on because doing so will only give too much importance and energy to the problems. You have to rise above the emotional level of consciousness to make it easier for you to understand what you are going through on a deeper level.

The process allows you to focus on your personal history, qualities you were familiar with but choose to ignore most of the time. These qualities emit certain colors shown in your outer aura.

These colors include the following:

- Blue signifies wisdom, love, perception, and intuition.

- Red signifies willpower, courage, leadership, and independence.

- Violet signifies dignity, truth, vitality, action, integrity, and rituals.

- Orange signifies beauty, balance, rhythm, and harmony

- Green signifies adaptability, mental power, impartiality, and instinctual power

- Yellow signifies patience, tolerance, precision, and logic.

- Rose pink signifies service to others, devotion, directness, and loyalty.

Meditation helps beginners in finding their unique quality color and meaning. Sound affects your energy fields. Sound healing operates within the laws of attraction, truth, love, and karmic cause and effect.

A part of the wider law of attraction states that lower vibration draws in a higher vibration. A second law states that higher vibration helps in bringing the lower vibration up to its own level. A third law follows the order in spiritual healing and the fourth law works by moving the energy in an upward manner once freed and transformed.

The fastest-moving energy in a human body is spiritual energy. You can easily draw it out whenever you need it to turn the vibrations from your emotional blockage into a lower frequency. The blockage comes from your old belief structures, the pent-up thought patterns, and emotions that formed vicious cycles.

To break the cycle, you need a higher understanding and a higher vibration. The blockage can resist consciousness, so you tend to carry them every day like excess baggage causing unwanted stress and tension. Through sound healing, your consciousness experiences a boost in energy that activates a temporary opening.

With activated energy, your consciousness follows the sound formed by a higher vibration. It observes the activation process. With the combined healing power of sound and the fast spiritual energies – truth, compassion, and love, your consciousness go through the process called consciousness growth. At this point, the consciousness learns to transform your old beliefs from a mental level and energy is freed once done.

If the process is accomplished through energy exercises or meditation, you will likely hear a popping sound that signifies the dissolution of a vicious cycle. The process is not easy since the energy fields are connected to the other levels of consciousness.

Effects of Sound

To maximize the benefits of sound healing, you have to tap the five important factors that determine the effects of sounds:

1. The receptivity of the receiver and being open to everything that might transpire during the process

2. The musical components used in the healing process

3. The attraction level of the person performing the healing session

4. The energies present while healing is going on, including people, time of day and year, and place.

5. The quality of the source of sound or the musical instruments used to facilitate the process.

Sound has multiple effects. First, the effect will depend on your background and how you respond emotionally to the sound. Sound will penetrate through the energy blockage and activate some of your subconscious memories. These memories range from visual scenes, karmic memories, emotions, sounds, and etheric-sensual. When you are ready, these memories will be brought into your consciousness. The healer will use different levels of sound until the vicious cycle is broken.

By releasing energy blockage, you will become more prepared for more changes and it also implies a change of attitude. Your aura and the aura of the healer will blend into a deeper level that will lead to the development of openness. The deeper the level that you can work with the healer, the more efficient the healing process will become.

Aside from the memories, sound healing can also help you in reaching the deeper levels of consciousness. This will give you a vision of what you want to become in this life, your dreams, and ambitions.

Sound healing is not a substitute for medicine. It heals the levels of your being that medicines cannot penetrate. It harmonizes the different areas of your being to make you feel complete. You will not readily feel the effects of the sound healing process. It takes about 24 to 36 hours after the treatment before you realize the changes.

Music has an important role in sound healing. By learning about what inspired its creation, the music will affect the different layers of your consciousness:

- Spiritual level – soul
- Upper astral – love, peace, serenity, joy, and compassion
- Lower astral – painful emotions
- Upper mental – intuition
- Lower mental – the level of intellect affected by the lower astral
- Collective layers – spiritual and collective memory

The five-element tool will come in handy to benefit from sound and music healing. Here's a look at the five elements and their role in the sound healing process:

1. Earth

In music, you will hear the earth quality in musical structures used as the foundation of any piece of song or music. When you play an instrument while your earth structure is imbalanced, the sound will lack security and confidence.

Some samples of the associated instruments with the earth element include sound bed, deep drums, deep voice of Tibetan singing monks, okarina, gongs, log drum, gong drum, ribbons of bells, didgeridoo, tampura, flowerpots, and electric or double bass, Indian surbahar, and cello.

2. Water

In music, this element is expressed on how the changing rhythms adapt to the sound – from the performance to the emotions it emits from the performer and listener. This element is associated with musical instruments that include clay pot drums, talking drums, and the Irish bodhran. It will also help to participate in trance-like rituals to re-establish your connection with the water element.

3. Fire

The element is expressed in music in a dynamic manner. This is done by playing a gong, drum or cymbals. You can also use your own voice to practice playing louder and softer sounds. You will need certain elements of the other areas to control fire in a productive manner. For fuel and strength, you will need the container that the earth element provides. You will need the water element to extinguish the fire and the air element to stimulate it.

Some of the musical instruments associated with the fire element include cymbals, woodblock, temple blocks, singing bowls used in a percussive manner, overtone flute, claves, kokiriko gekko, rattles, crystal bowls, horns, wooden clap, saxophone, trumpet, and Indian shanai.

4. Air

In music, the feeling of this element is brought about by the striking chords and the big movements of a melody, compels your body to dance and raise your hands. Flutes and strings are some samples of the instruments of the air element. To get a sense of fulfillment and joy, you'll need to find the kind of instrument that best describes who you are.

Some of the musical instruments associated with the air element include Japanese singing bowls, sound bed, tubular bells, hang, koto-monochord, flutes, tambura, glockenspiel, aeolian harp, bar chimes, harp, zither, birds song, synthesizer, violin, Indian sitar, and hammered dulcimer

5. Space

This element is heard in music used in meditation, overtone chanting, the Tibetan singing bowls, Gregorian chant, and use of gongs. It is also common for recording studios to use the reverberation and echo effects in their music.

Uses of Sound and Music Healing

There are two distinct areas of sound healing: the utilization of sound for medical purposes and the use of music for learning, relaxation, and productivity. Different techniques and musical instruments are used to facilitate the healing process, but the human voice is said to be the most powerful among all the instruments.

Sound healing is used for different purposes, which include the following:

1. Pain Alleviation

Sound is used in the birthing process using a wide range of songs that help in making the birthing process smoother and less painful for the mother. The technique is also used in the dying process where music and sound are played to aid to a beautiful death.

Many doctors around the world utilize sound therapy before, during, and after an operation procedure. The technique has shown a substantial reduction in the amount of anesthesia used in the practice.

2. Voice Analysis

It utilizes multiple systems to provide a blueprint of what's going on inside your body. The frequencies in the voice provide a map of the different aspects of your being – emotional, mental, spiritual, and physical.

Voice analysis can help in detecting the ailing organs in the body and the presence of any signs of diseases. These health issues are addressed using music and specific sounds.

3. Therapeutic benefits of sound

The importance of sound in healing is now being used in many complementary and integrative healing centers. Their services include relaxation techniques, reduction of hearing sensitivities, stimulation of the nervous system and brain, auditory biofeedback, and stress management. They also use sound and music to correct learning problems and making the auditory tonal processing better.

4. Uses of sound in the medical field

The medical field, despite the continuous technological advancement, is utilizing sound in healing. Sound is utilized in various techniques, including sound massage, sound surgery and the use of sound inside the body. Ultrasound has been used for many years in breaking up plaque on teeth and kidney stones.

There are ongoing studies to find out more about how the cell opens up to receive energy once the resonant frequency of a cell is found. The cell explodes when the resonant frequency's volume is raised. Medical practitioners utilize certain non-invasive medical techniques to destroy diseased cells without side effects. One sample of this technique is the use of highly precise tones in the targeted organs of the body.

The experts are now geared towards finding more options on how sound can heal. It follows the basic notion that people only need to accept and learn how to use their power to heal themselves with the aid of sound and music.

5. Learning how to connect with one's spirit and raise consciousness through music and sound. Sound healing allows you to discover your inner thoughts and desire, including what makes you happy and contented.

Chapter 15 - Vibrational Healing

It follows the concept that everything that surrounds you vibrates. The human body works with several rhythms, such as:

1. Cranio-sacral pulse – the pressure of the liquid in the brain and spinal cord that pulses 8 to 12 times per minute.

2. Brain waves – The normal rate when you are awake is 18 to 22 cycles per second.

3. Breath – an average person breathes 14 to 16 times per minute.

4. Stomach – contracts every 3 minutes.

5. Heart – resting heart rate is 60 beats per minute, heart rate after doing average activity is 72 beats per minute, and the normal heart rate is 60 to 70 beats per minute.

6. Gastrointestinal tract – contracts one time per minute.

7. Body temperature – changes from day to night.

The practices done during a healing session, including sound and music, affect the rhythms. You'll have up to 87 heartbeats per minute when stressed and about 57 heartbeats per minute when relaxed.

Here are some samples of the instruments and techniques used in sound healing:

- Vocal expression – chanting, singing, toning, and laughing
- Relaxing and therapeutic music
- Self-healing
- Healing facilitated by a sound healer
- Different musical instruments

Like many kinds of alternative medicine, sound healing doesn't have the same effects on everyone. Your healing depends on many factors, including the techniques used and how open you are about the process.

Here are some samples of the known benefits of sound healing:

- Enhances your immune system
- Corrects the body's imbalances
- Improves brain function
- Helps in giving you a more positive outlook in life
- Makes it easier for you to deal with problems and other challenges in life

- Helps you understand your emotions on a deeper level
- Tunes the auric field and your physical state to resonate in harmony with your surroundings
- Removes the feeling of emptiness and makes it easier for you to feel whole
- Improves mood and sleeping pattern
- Reduces headaches and migraine attack
- Shrinking of ovarian cysts
- Reduced inflammation and improved joint function
- Helps in healing bunions and kidney stones
- Modification of the heart rate, blood pressure, breathing depth, and breathing rate
- Deep relaxation and stress alleviation
- Relieves anxiety and depression
- Triggers the release of endorphin responsible for pain reduction and enhanced mood
- Allows the body to heal on its own

Overall, sound healing makes you happier and healthier. It improves your mood, outlook on life, energy, and wisdom.

The Other Aspects of Sound Healing

For sound healing to work, you have to trust sounds and let them into your consciousness. Only then will they be able to penetrate your core and dissolve the blockage causing your illness and depression.

Here are some vital tips on how to maximize the benefits of the process:

1. You can use recorded music in sound healing, something played using single or only a few instruments.

2. Lie down or sit during the process. You have to be comfortable without falling asleep. Wear loose clothing and take off your shoes.

3. The left side of the brain or the intellectual side takes up to 20 minutes to calm down. Do not hurry the process. The right side of the brain will naturally take over and when it happens, you'll become more aware of the healing process.

4. Perform a relaxation exercise before the healing process. You can do slow and fluid movements along with soft and deep breathing, which will help in improving your overall body contact.

5. Consider the process as your "me time". Disengage from anything that will distract your thoughts.

The Effects of Sound

It will take up to 36 hours or more to feel the effects of sound depending on the sound used in the process. It goes deep into the energy fields surrounding your body and leaves traces. Sound affects your psycho-energetic system in many different ways.

The rhythm of a deep hand drum, for example, affects the lower part of the body – from the pelvic area to your feet. It emits emotional and mental reactions. If the instrument was intentionally played to make you feel inspired, the effects will become visible in your outer aura. You may feel and realize the effects of your dreams. You will also develop inner changes without being aware that it is happening.

Sound with penetrative effects in your etheric energy field comes from hard percussion instruments, such as gongs, bells, Tibetan bowls, cymbals, or bells, glass, and tubular bells. For a more potent effect, the instrument has to be played using a hard object made of hard rubber or wood.

The sounds from the instruments go deep into the two layers of the etheric in your body – the light ether and chemical. To prevent any blockage, it will help if you'll perform the right energy awareness exercises along with the penetrative sounds.

The etheric energy field is not exclusive to humans. Everything around you – animals, objects, plants, air, planets, has it. The shape of an instrument affects the sound form and helps in realizing the resting center found in your core.

The sound form next to the instrument used is recognized as a physical phenomenon, which is felt like a density or pressure. Its energy form spreads and extends along with the shape and could sometimes be sensed at a distance. You will feel the instrument quality on a spiritual level.

A musical instrument has a memory of how it was played and who handled it. Through time, it will accumulate different levels of energy. This is the reason why it takes several playtimes before a new musical instrument can develop its full potential.

Chapter 16 - Healing Instruments

There are many musical instruments used for healing. They represent one or a combination of the five phases of energy change, which include the following:

1. Earth – clay instruments associated with structured thinking, spleen, and the stomach

2. Metal – normal or tubular bells associated with depression, sadness, and lungs

3. Water – drums linked to fear and the kidneys

4. Wood – instruments made of wood associated with will, anger, and liver

5. Fire – stringed musical instruments associated with the heart and happiness

Here's a comprehensive list of the instruments used in sound healing:

String Instruments

They gravitate to the air element. The strings that produce low notes will settle towards the bottom of the torso and the types that produce high notes will keep your attention to the chest area. In traditional Chinese medicine, these instruments are used in treating heart-related problems.

1. Guitar

It plays a perfect chord by simply striking the strings and without an elaborate left-hand technique. You can hear water with the changing flow of the sound of the guitar. The earth's qualities are attracted to its rhythmical base. The air element is drawn when the instrument is played in a melodic manner.

2. Violin

Its sound affects the body along the lower ribs in between the heart chakra and the solar plexus. It draws the air element by opening up the upper half of your chest. The sound will emit the feeling of inspiration, especially with the way your shoulders and arms move.

3. Harp

The sound helps a person to go into deep relaxation. It calms the nervous system and opens your mental field. The massively generated notes due to the 6 octaves of strings a concert harp has make this an instrument of angels. The sound feels as if you are being lifted, which no other instrument can make.

4. Sithar

The complex technique of how it is played attracts strong air. You will hear the sympathetic strings resound every time you play a note in this melodic instrument.

5. Sound bed

This therapeutic instrument will require you to lie down in a hollow table, which is actually a large monochord. It has about 50 strings beneath the table tuned according to the patient's needs. The sound bed and the monochord affect the senses by making them sharper and they also soothe the nervous system. The bed will move you towards the element of space. It also emits a motherly-like sound that will draw you towards the qualities of the earth. You'll feel drawn to the fire element when the sound bed and monochord are played using mallets.

6. Tampura

This instrument has four strings tuned to two identical fifths, octave, and tonica. It establishes an earth sound, or a drone background used in Indian classical music. It has similarities with sithar but it cannot play melodies. To produce a range of overtones of air, fire, and space, a string of cotton is inserted on the end of its string. The sound it emits is both reassuring and calming.

7. Cello

When played in lower notes, your focus will be drawn towards the water area or your pelvic and hips and fire area or your navel. When you play it in a freestyle manner, you will develop sensitivity to its sound and proper intonation.

Drums

Drums activate the water and earth elements.

1. Clay Pot Drums

They help in directing your focus to the belly area. They create a soft and low pitch when the hole is slapped using your hand.

2. Ocean Drums

The instrument has numerous tiny metal marbles inside the double frame drums. By rolling the drums in different directions, you will hear a sound similar to the waves on the beach. It helps in calming babies as the sound will remind them of the blood moving inside their mother's aorta while they were still unborn.

3. Water drum

This instrument produces soft percussive sound when the upper calebasse is knocked with a soft mallet. Press the upper bowl near or far from the water to create varying pitches.

4. Talking drum

Place the instrument under your armpit and squeeze to produce varying pitches depending on how hard you squeeze it. You can also play the instrument using a mallet or your fingers. This drum produces a soft watery sound.

5. Slid or log drum

This rectangular closed box made of wood instrument is more of a xylophone than a drum. The cavity emits a warm sound. You can play it using a hard material to attract earth and fire qualities and play using soft mallets to attract air and water.

6. Tabla

Considered as the most popular Indian percussion instrument, the smaller type activates the mental and fire aura while the larger drum attracts water qualities.

7. Bodhran

You can play this tunable instrument with your hand for a softer tone and to create a sound with more water and air. You can also play this using a double-edged wooden beater to create a harder tone.

Small Percussion

1. Indonesian Kokiriko Gekko, Wooden Claps

They create a dry and sharp sound that attracts the fire area.

2. Chicken Shake, Maracas, Rattles, Chakchas

They emit sounds that loosen the etheric and get rid of the energy blockage. They help in making you more alert and in stimulating your nervous system.

3. Rainstick

When used while seated, it creates a relaxing sound, especially when placed near the back, shoulders, or neck.

4. Claves

The instrument, made of a pair of short hardwood sticks, produces a dry, awakening, and sharp sound when hit together. It attracts the earth element when played with regular pulsations. In traditional Chinese medicine, it is used to tap a person's fire element.

5. Tempelblocks, Woodblocks, Wooden bells

When hit with hard mallets, these tuned instruments produce a sharp and dry sound that brings you towards heightened consciousness when played during meditation. Use your bare hands in playing the instruments to create a warmer sound.

Tuned percussion

1. Crystal Singing Bowls

Rub or bang the bowls with different mallets to create a penetrative sound used for healing.

2. Mouth Harp

This old instrument can induce trance. To make different sounds, change the size of the cavity of your mouth, position of your tongue, or the style of your breathing.

3. Bass xylophone bars

They offer the most beautiful and warmest sounds among any wooden instruments.

4. Boom Whackers

The instrument made of short tubes of plastic is played by slapping them on your thigh to make a sound.

5. Flowerpots

They are lithophones that produce beautiful earthly sounds.

6. Lithophones

They produce a pure sound that invokes the power of the sky. The sound is not earthly but more on cold, brilliant, and dry.

Keyboards

1. Piano

The instrument also attract water, fire, space, air, and earth qualities depending on the piece that you are playing.

2. Waterphone

This new instrument can create unfamiliar and new sounds.

Wind Instruments – Flutes

1. Pan Flute

The instrument is easy to play. Every note has its own bamboo tube and it emits a smokey sound. It comes in different forms, such as a double row, straight row, and bent.

2. Overtone Flute

The instrument doesn't require any fingering technique and can be easily played by people of all ages and even those with disabilities. You can make varying sounds depending on how strong or soft your blow is.

4. Didgeridoo

The original instrument was made of wood from the eucalyptus tree. Once you learn how to play this right, it can help in improving your grounding and it also increases your awareness of the earth element. You need to do a circular breathing technique to play the instrument.

5. Bullroarer

It has a low roaring sound that draws the solar plexus. Whirl the string attached to a piece of flat wood around your head to create a sound.

6. Ocarina

Considered as one of the oldest flutes, this instrument made of clay emits a damp and warm sound. The warm tone and simple melodies will help you in connecting with your feelings.

7. Irish Whistle

This metallic instrument has six holes that can play a full musical scale. You will need more than one whistle to produce sounds of different keys.

8. Low Whistle

This instrument made of aluminum can be played with a range of subtlety. You will need to play it in front of a microphone to hear it clearly.

9. Saxophone

Its sound draws your attention to your stomach and sternum. The sound also draws you closer to light, warmth, and fire.

10. Bird's Voices

Various instruments that emit songs of different birds are now available. The sound will remind you of nature and has calming and soothing effects.

11. Conch

Considered as one of the oldest instruments and is played by blowing in its opening. It is made of a sea shell with the tip cut off. The sound it emits is haunting and reverberates in places, like a cave, rocky walls, and church. To create varying sounds, you will need to change the tension of your lips.

Metallophones

1. Table Tubes

The instrument made of a set of tuned tubular bells arranged in a frame is played using a medium felt ball mallet.

2. Glockenspiel

This metal instrument is a cousin of the wooden xylophone. The best type among its kind is said to be the ones with lower tones and resonators.

3. Gongs

Gongs vary in size and sound but all of them create a powerful sound. The instruments are played with sensitivity in sound healing. It offers healing benefits to people with an oversensitive solar plexus zone.

4. Barchimes

It has several small metal chimes arranged in a declining order and hung on a horizontal piece of bamboo. To emit a sound that will draw your mental aura and nervous system, play the instrument by gliding any object or your hand along with the chimes.

5. Tubular Bells

The sound of the bells expands quickly up to a point when you will get confused where the sound is coming from. The sound lingers in the room for an extended period, a common characteristic of most metallic percussion instruments. When used to attract the element of space, the sound allows the expansion of the mental aura. It helps you in overcoming your vices, fears, and worries.

6. Windchimes

The instrument will create sound when hit by the wind. It will create a reinforcing effect when placed above the points where the energy lines meet.

7. Cymbals

It creates a powerful sound that brings out your fire quality, especially helpful to people with hypersensitive solar plexus. You can practice playing the cymbals at your own pace. Listen to how your body reacts to the sound and continue playing in ways that it affects your core. Do not play it too loud or else the sound will hit the nervous system directly and might cause a fright.

8. Small cymbals and bells

They come in pair that when hit together, create a metallic, penetrating, and sharp sound. They are capable of activating the space and air elements. You can activate the healing powers of the instruments by placing them above an acupuncture point. They have the ability to calm the energy, activate, or dissipate depending on how they are played.

9. Singing Bowls

The sound depends on the kind of singing bowls you play. They come in two basic forms – the traditional Himalayan singing bowl and the steel bowls from Japan, China, or Korea. The steel bowls sound sharp, clear, and straight. The Himalayan bowls produce a wavering sound.

You can play these bowls with the tip of your finger or by using the top mallets. To create a long constant sound, you can rub the bowls with a wooden beater. The sound makes a pleasant impression and helps you in finding your center.

Most Popular Instrument for Sound Healing in Buddhism

Tibetan singing bowls, also called Himalayan bowls, have long been used by Buddhist monks in their meditation practices. The instrument is also popularly used for healing by wellness practitioners, such as yoga therapists, massage therapists, and music therapists.

These singing bowls are categorized as a bell. The vibration of the bell when played, result in a deep and rich tone. Aside from the healing effects, these Tibetan singing bowls are also used to achieve deep relaxation.

The vibrations produced by the instrument is said to be beneficial in giving the energy system of the body its needed balance. It also harmonizes the cells and reduces stress.

To use the singing bowl for healing purposes, hold the mallet and press it in a circular motion at the bowl's rim. Use your arm instead of your wrist in accomplishing the motion. Slow down once you hear a clear and bright tone produced from the process. The other ways of playing the instrument include striking the bowl in a gentle manner before starting with the circular motion and performing the circular motion against the bowl's outside belly.

If you want to purchase the Tibetan singing bowls for healing purposes, look for high-quality materials capable of producing more resonant sounds. You can get them at specialty stores for new age products, music shops, yoga studios, certain meditation centers, and online shops.

Conclusion

I'd like to thank you and congratulate you for transiting my lines from start to finish.

I hope this book was able to help you understand the Buddha's sample and what you can do to follow his lead towards enlightenment.

The next step is to try different meditation practices, including proper exercises and breathing. All these will help you understand yourself better and all the things that surround you.

I know you could have picked any number of books to read, but you picked this book and for that I am extremely grateful.

If you enjoyed this book and found some benefit in reading this, I'd like to hear from you and hope that you could take some time to post a review. Your feedback and support will help this author to greatly improve his writing craft for future projects and make this book even better.

I want you, the reader, to know that your review is very important and so, if you'd like to leave a review, all you have to do is click here and away you go. I wish you all the best in your future success!

Thank you and good luck!

Harini Anand

A SPIRITUAL START!

Start your week with gratitude, joy, inspiration, and love.

Healing, motivation, inspiration, challenge and guidance straight to your inbox every week!

FIND OUT MORE

www.ingramcontent.com/pod-product-compliance
Lightning Source LLC
Chambersburg PA
CBHW021107080526
44587CB00010B/425